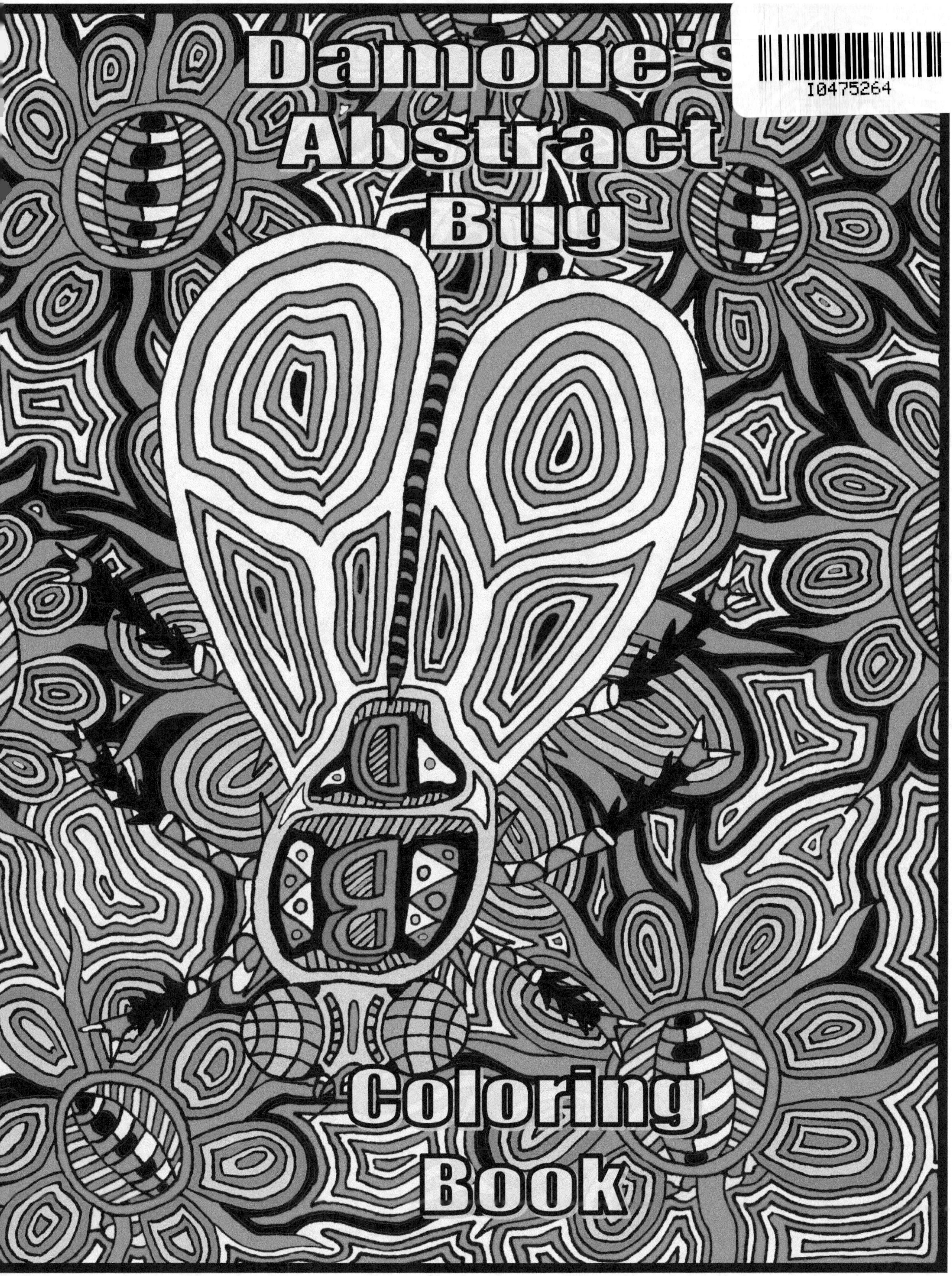
Damone's
Abstract
Bug
Coloring
Book

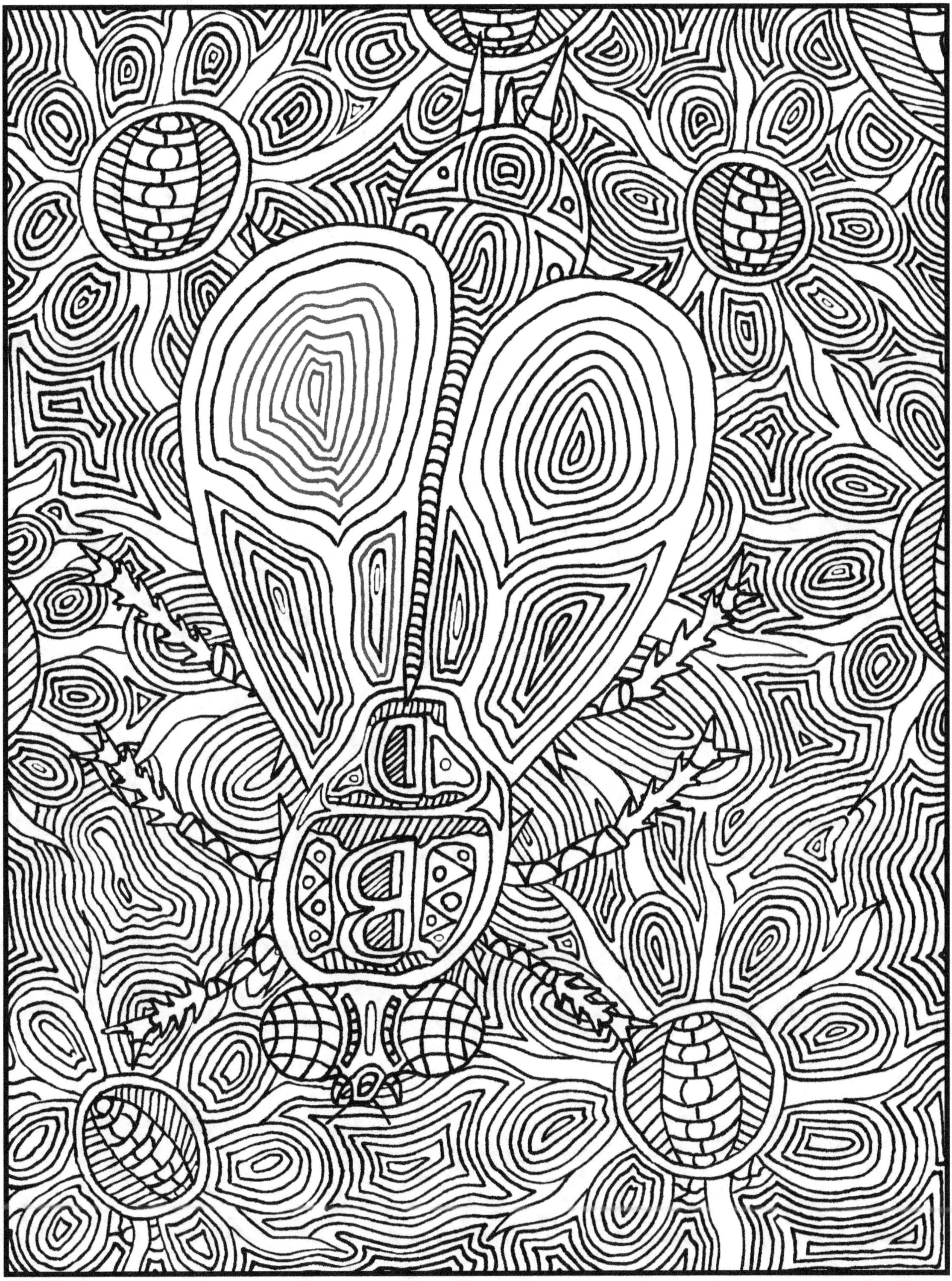

© Damone Heins

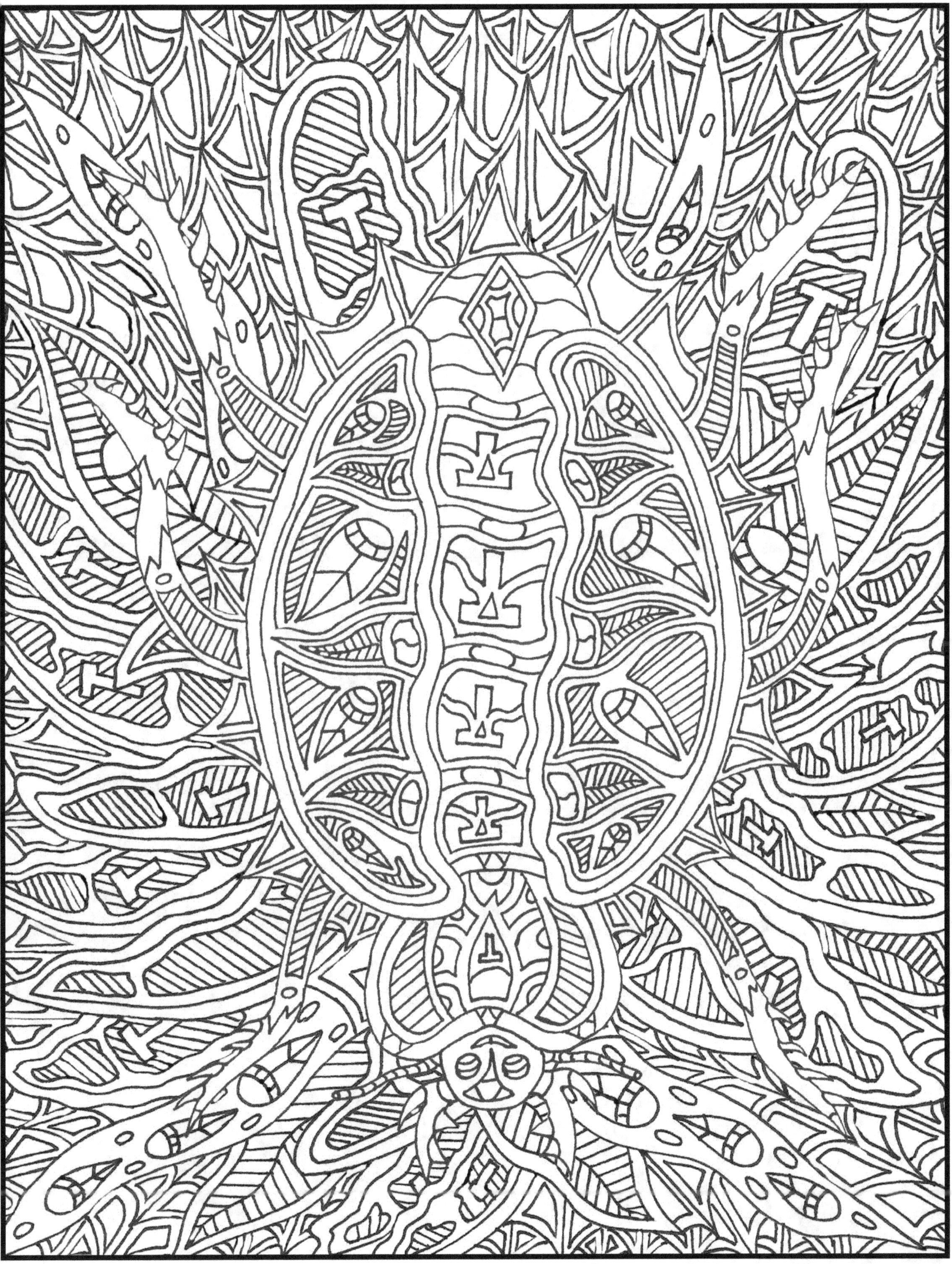

© Damone Heins

© Damone Heins

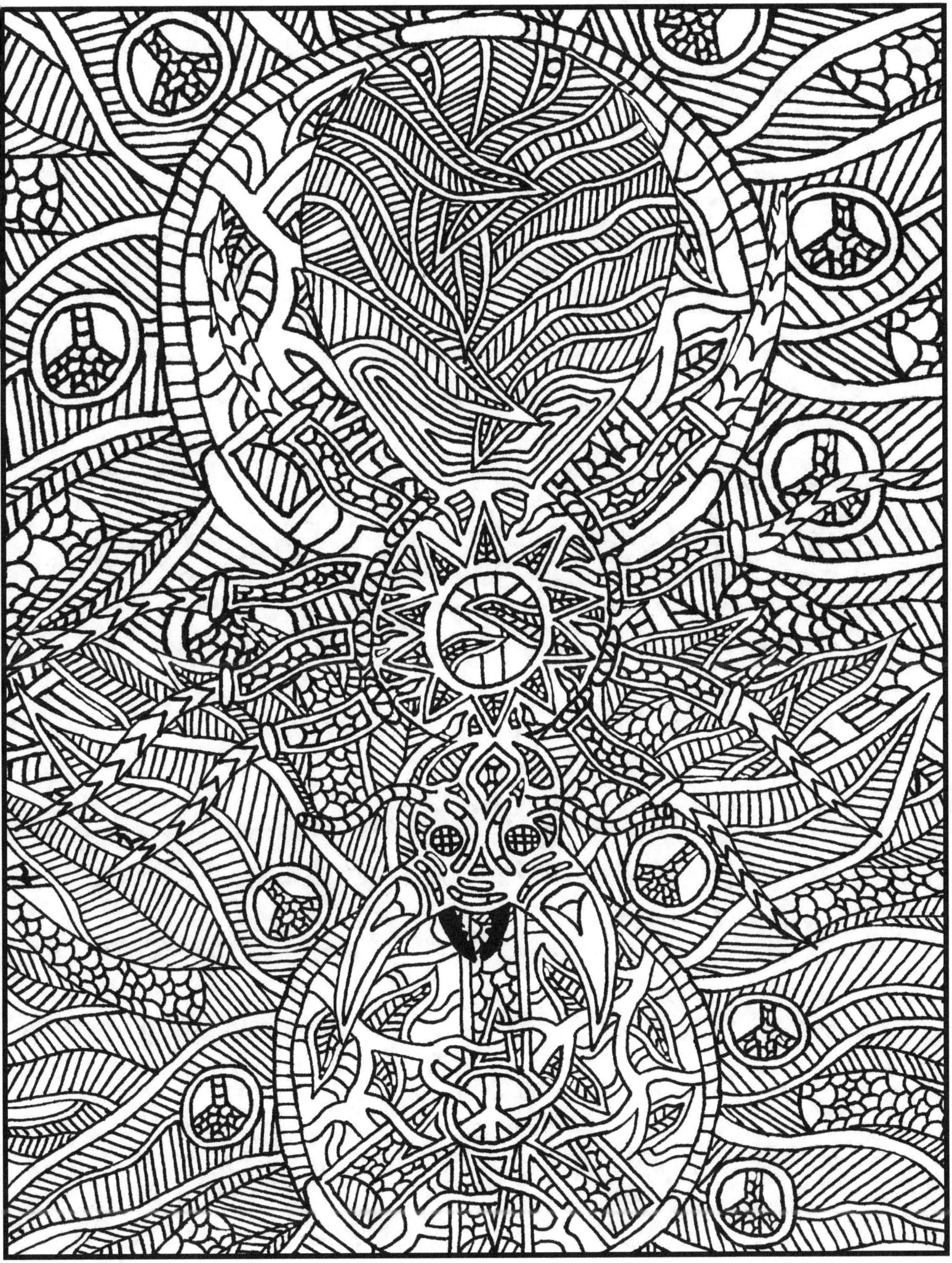

© Damone Heins

© Damone Heins

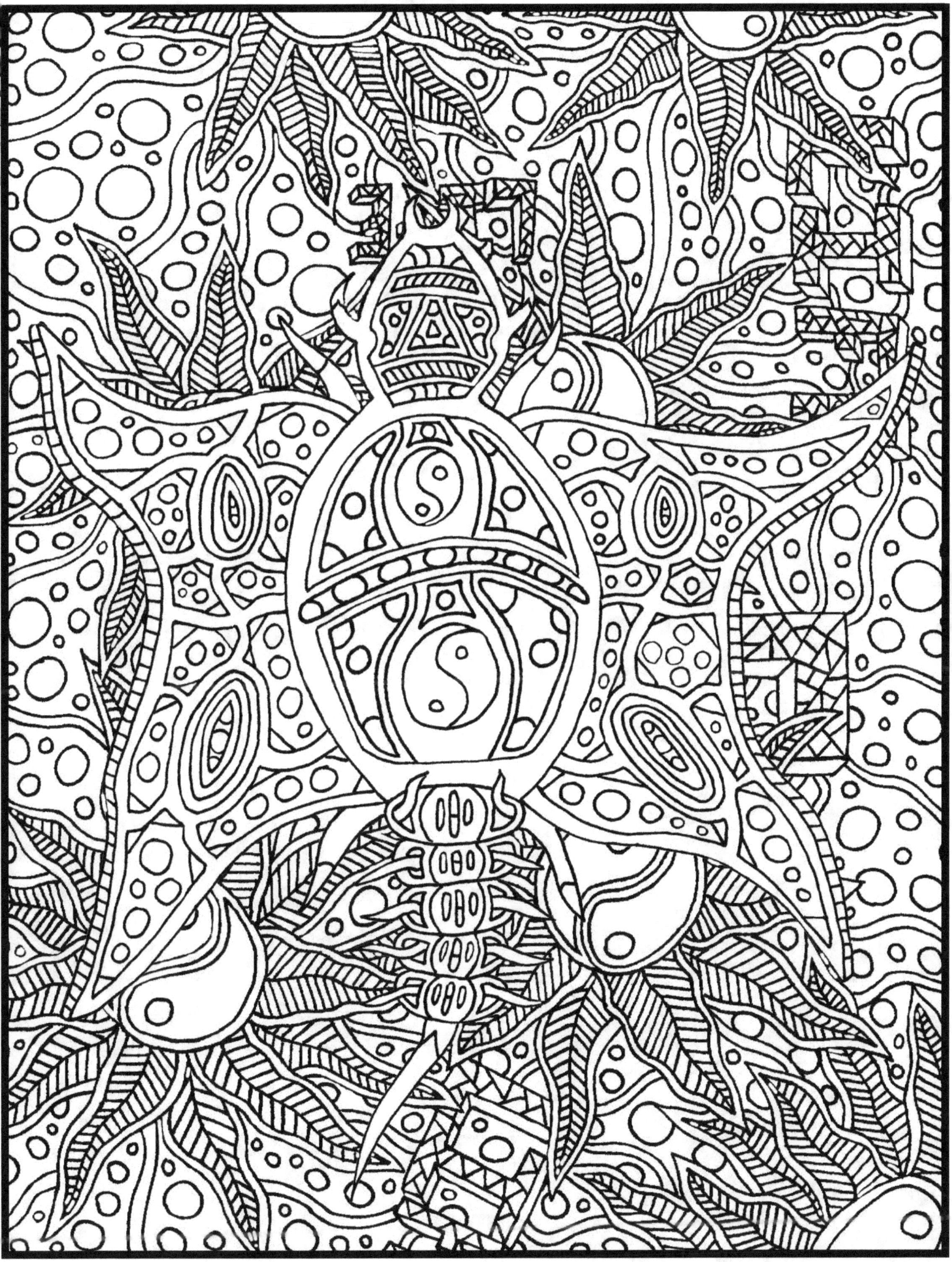

© Damone Heins

© Damone Heins

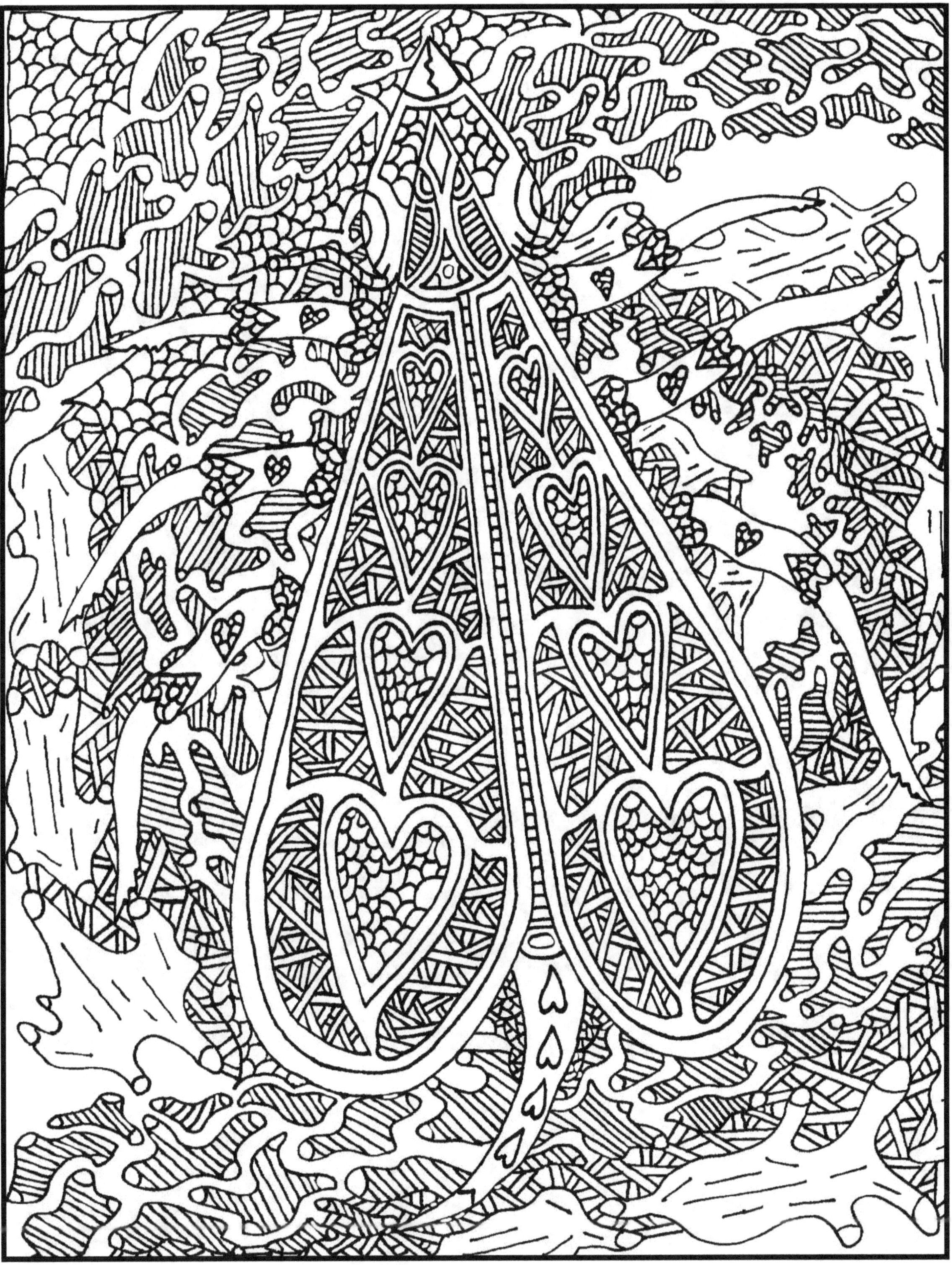

© Damone Heins

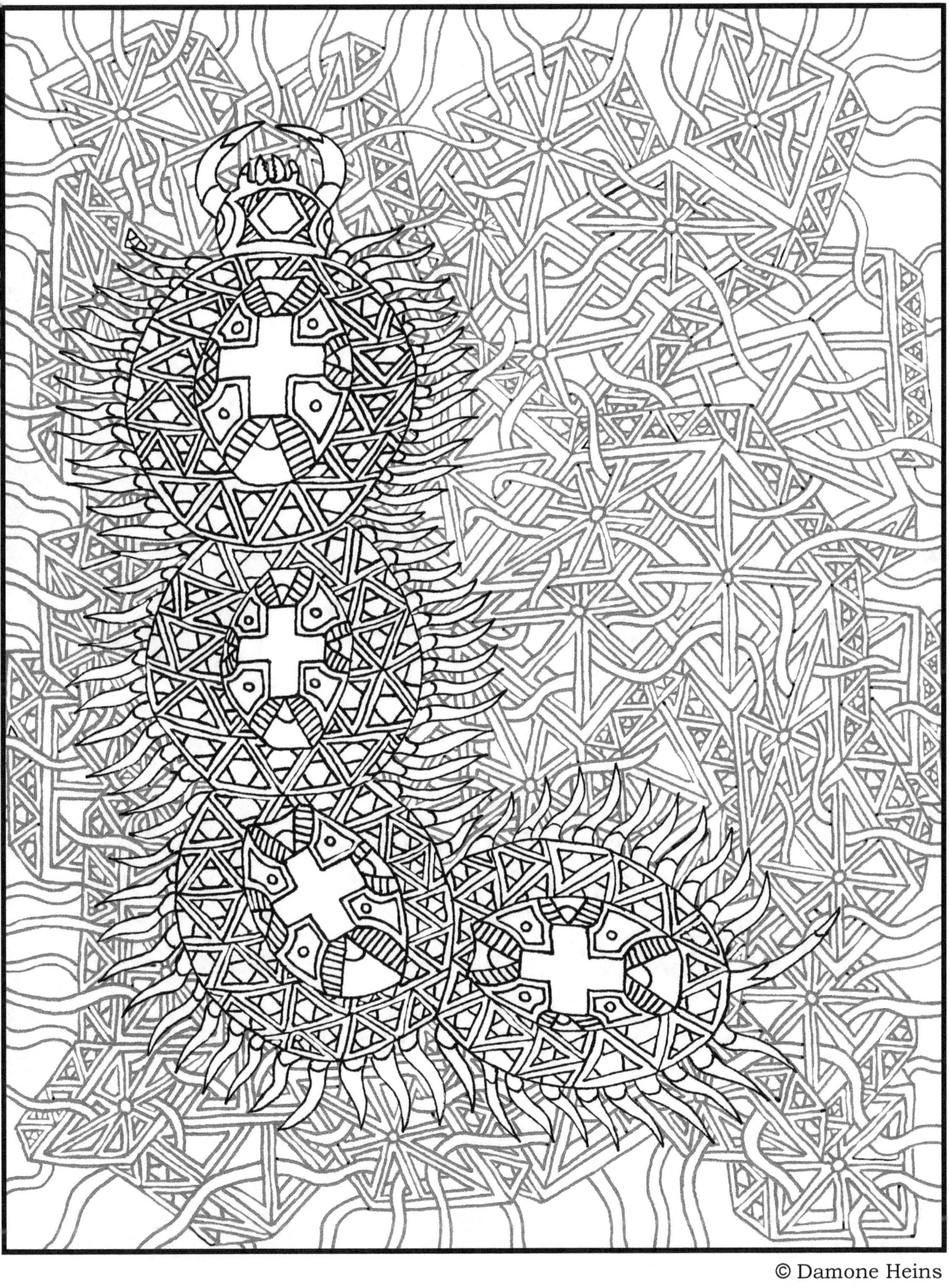

© Damone Heins

© Damone Heins

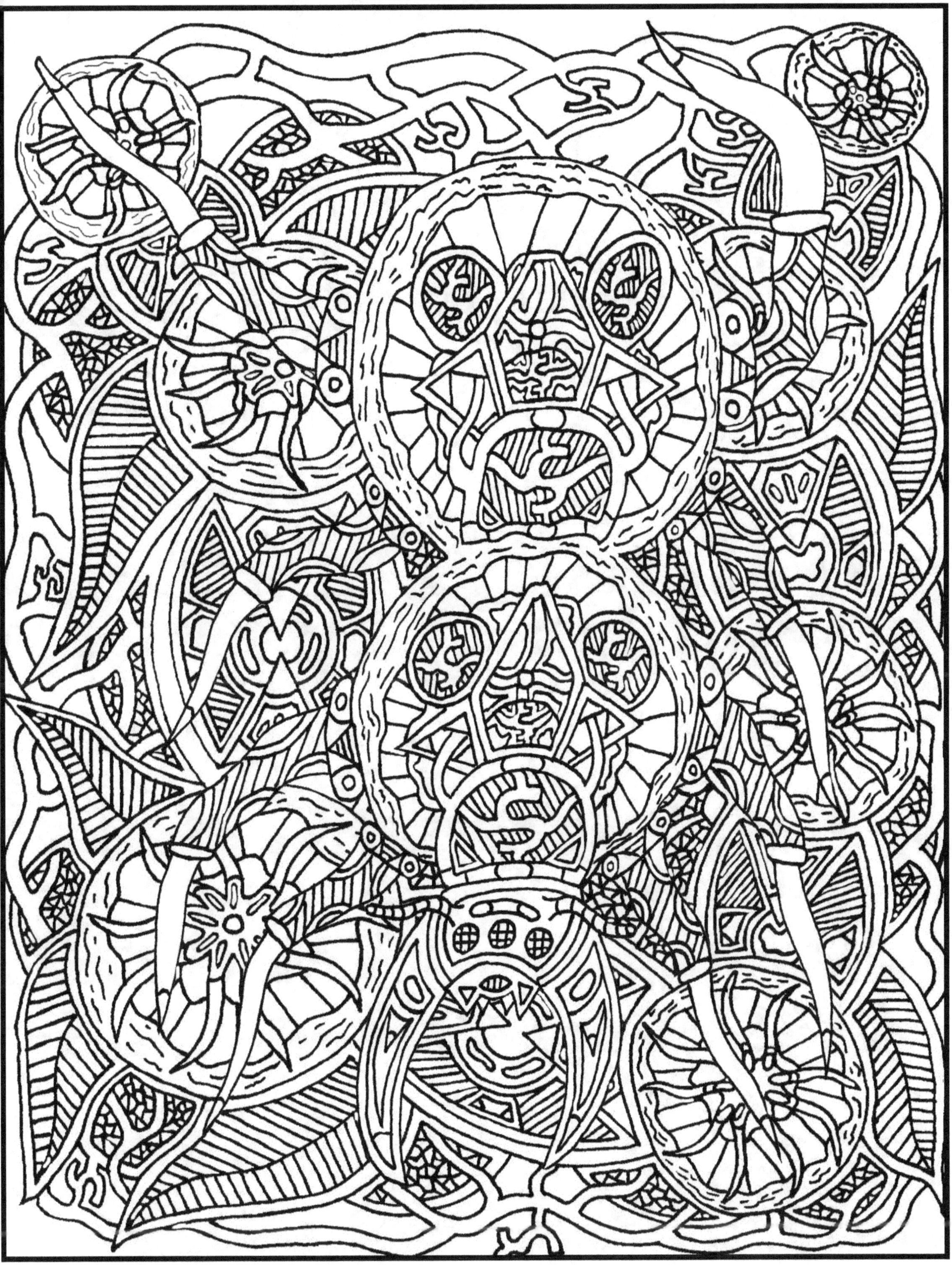

© Damone Heins

© Damone Heins

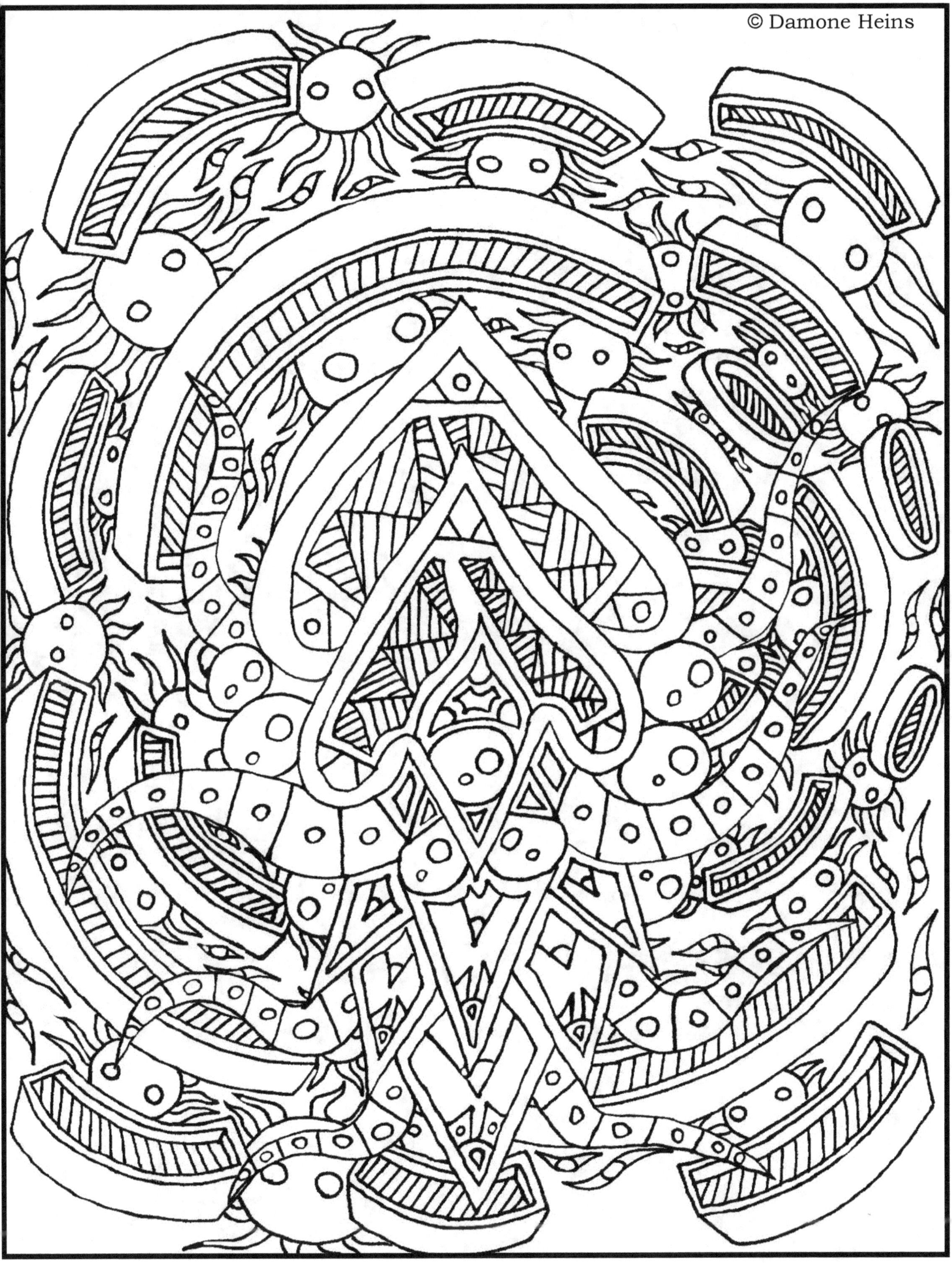
© Damone Heins

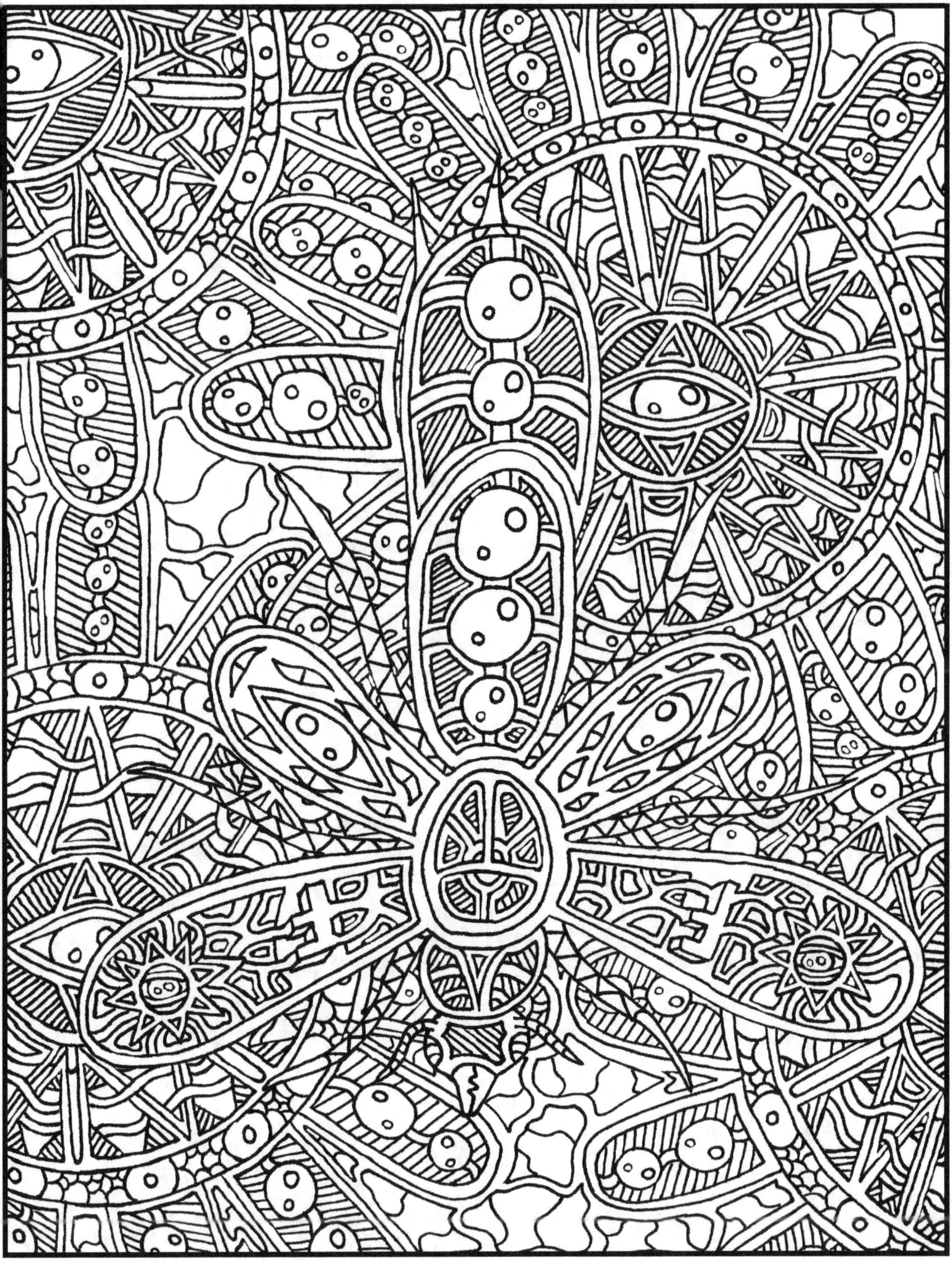

© Damone Heins

© Damone Heins

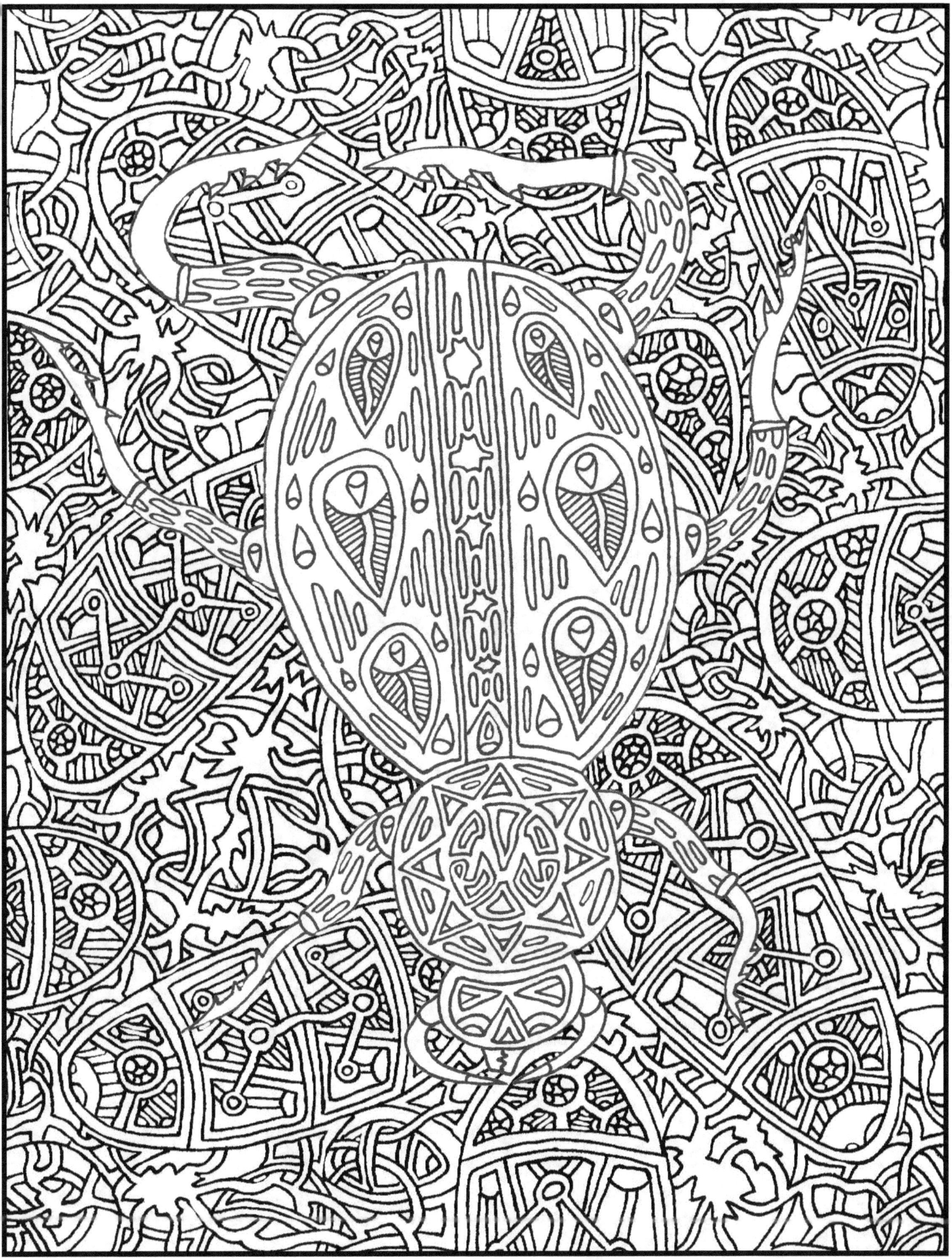

© Damone Heins

© Damone Heins

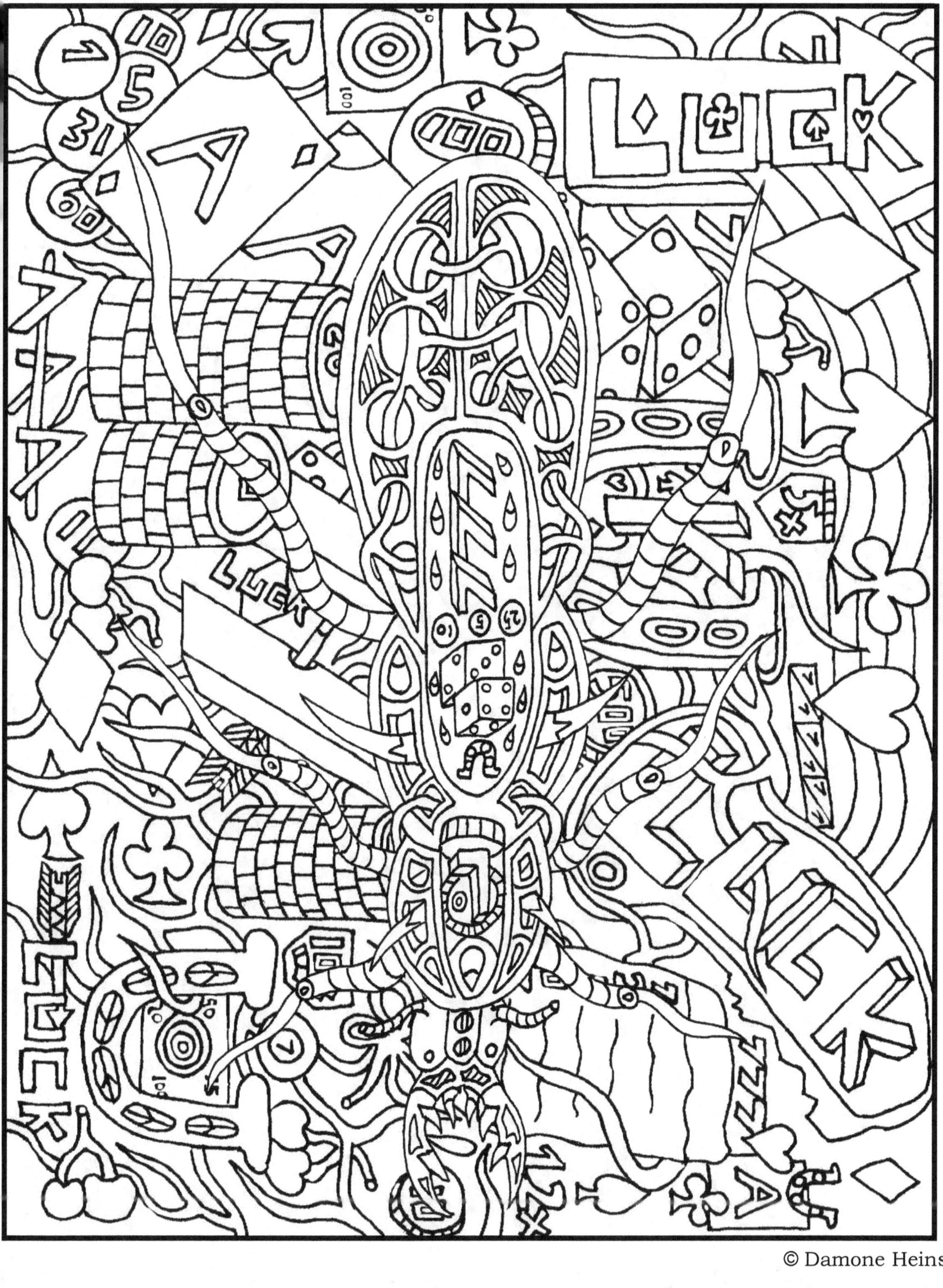

© Damone Heins

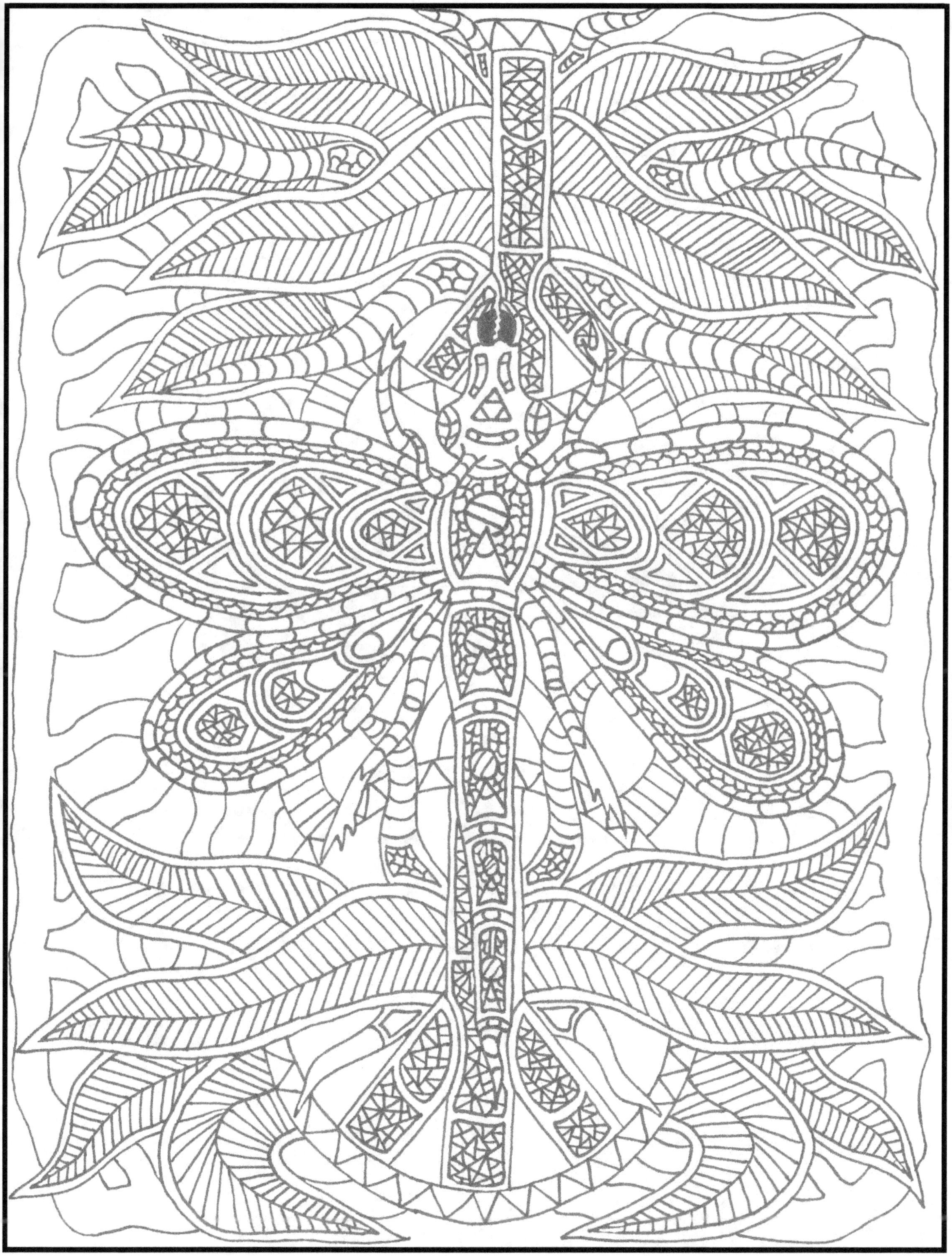

© Damone Heins

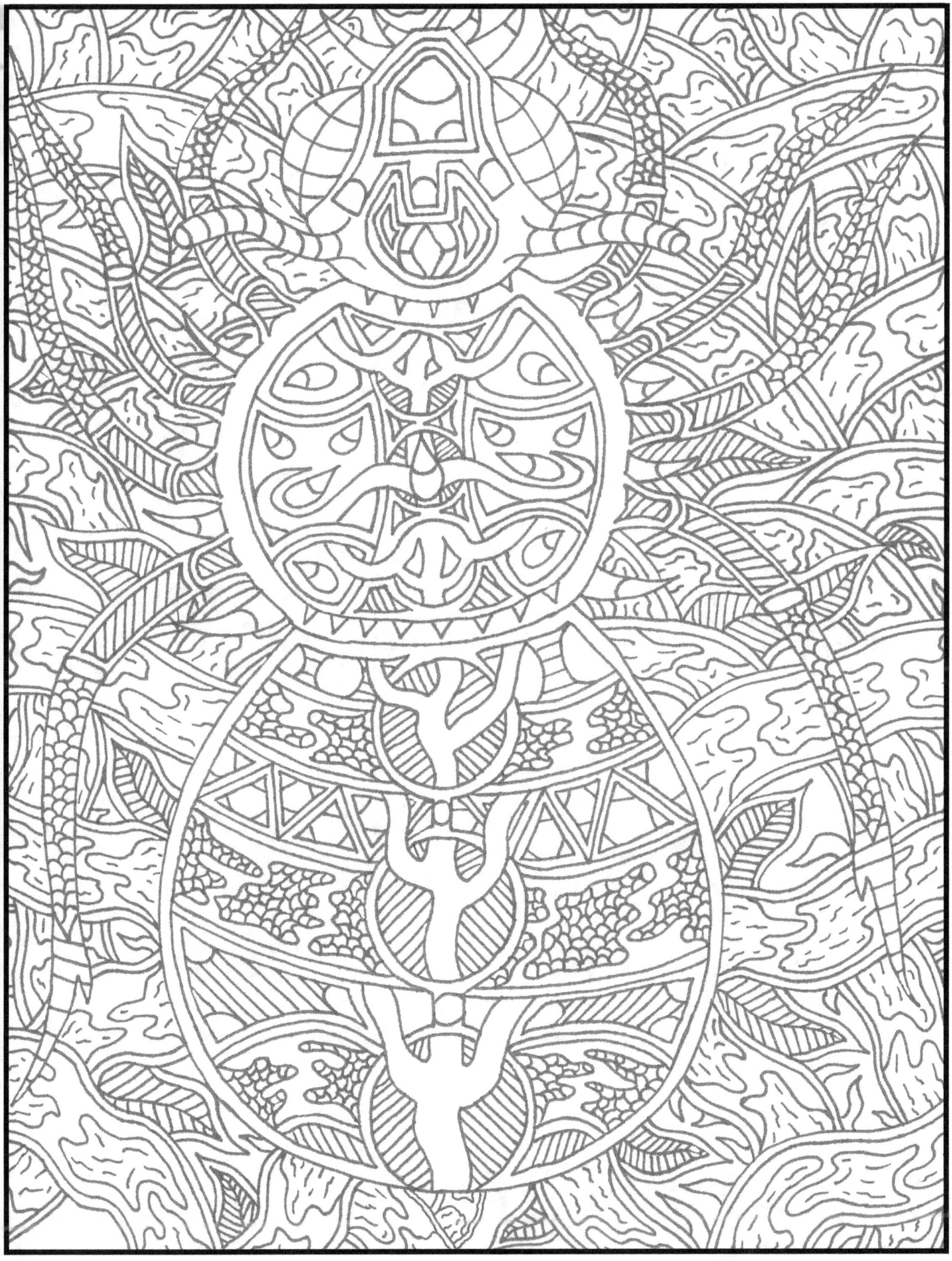
© Damone Heins

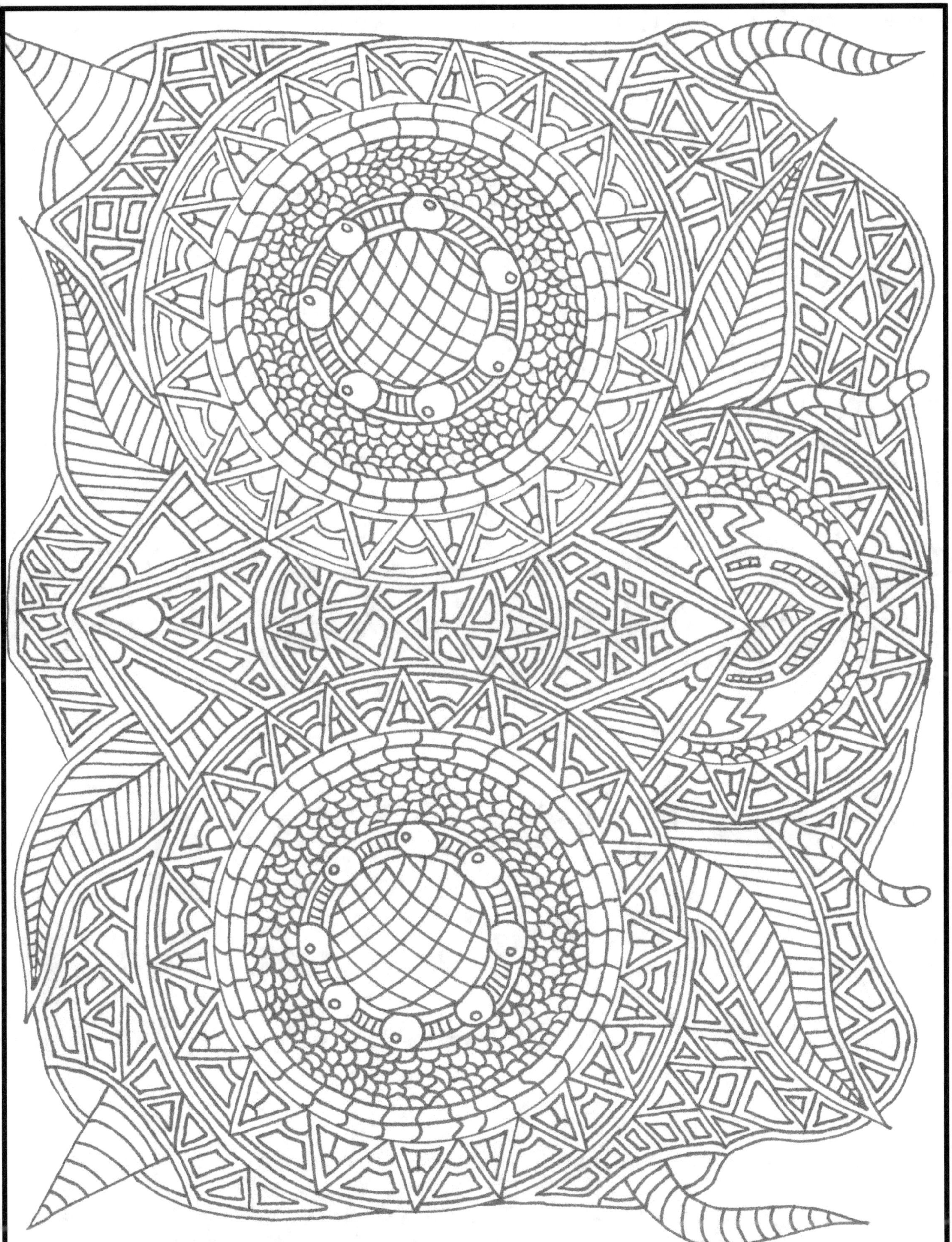

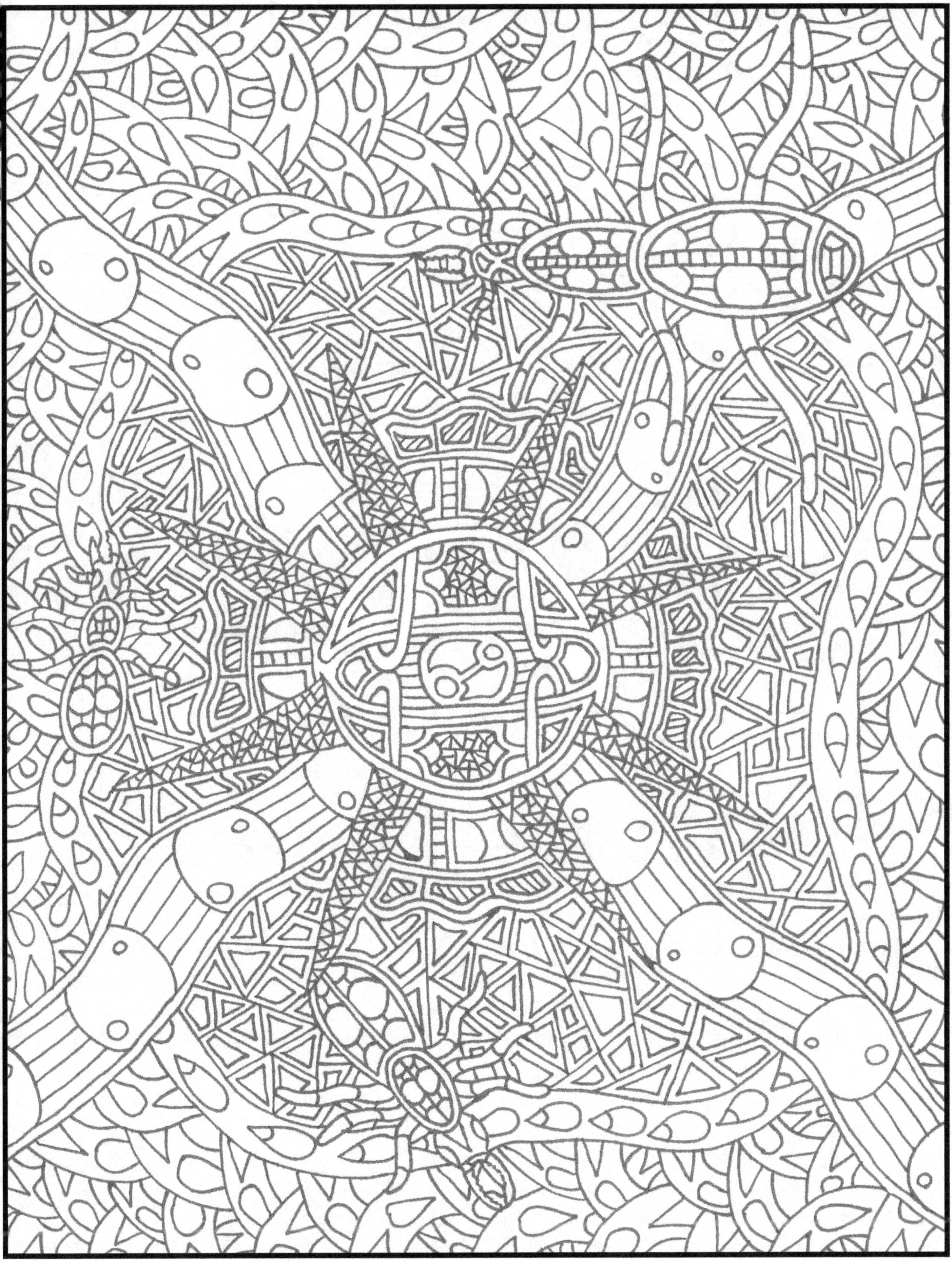

© Damone Heins

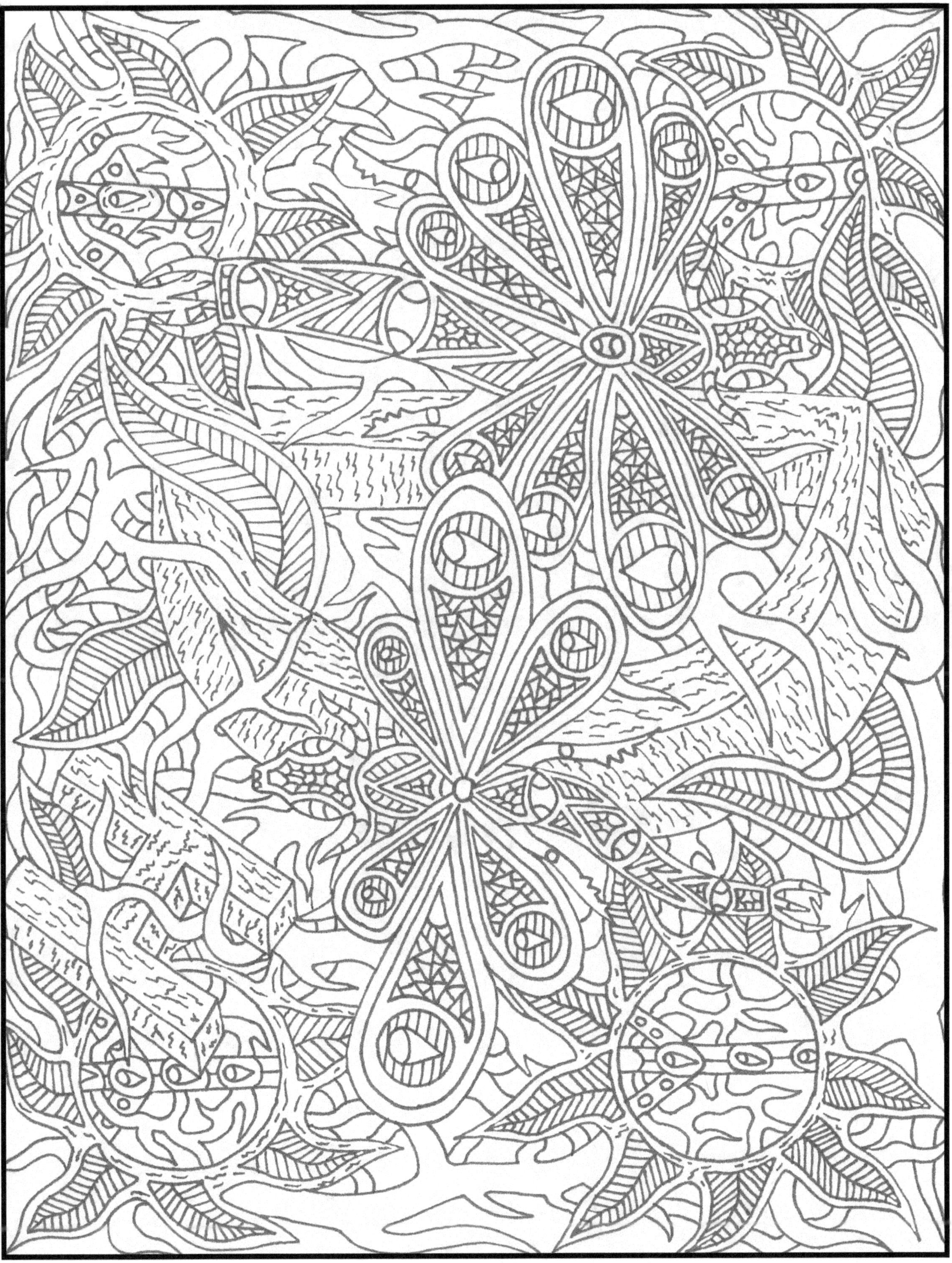

© Damone Heins

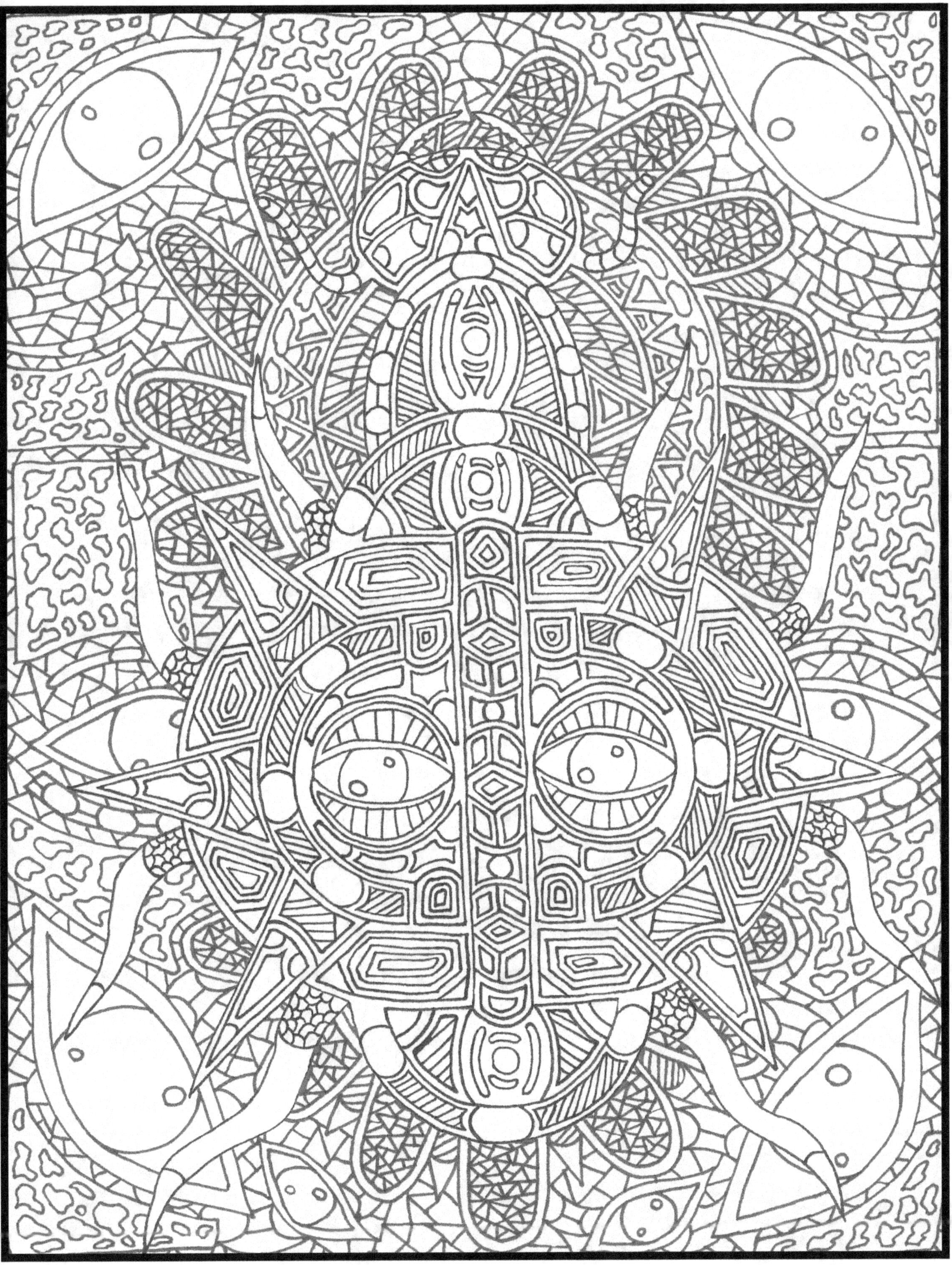

© Damone Heins

© Damone Heins

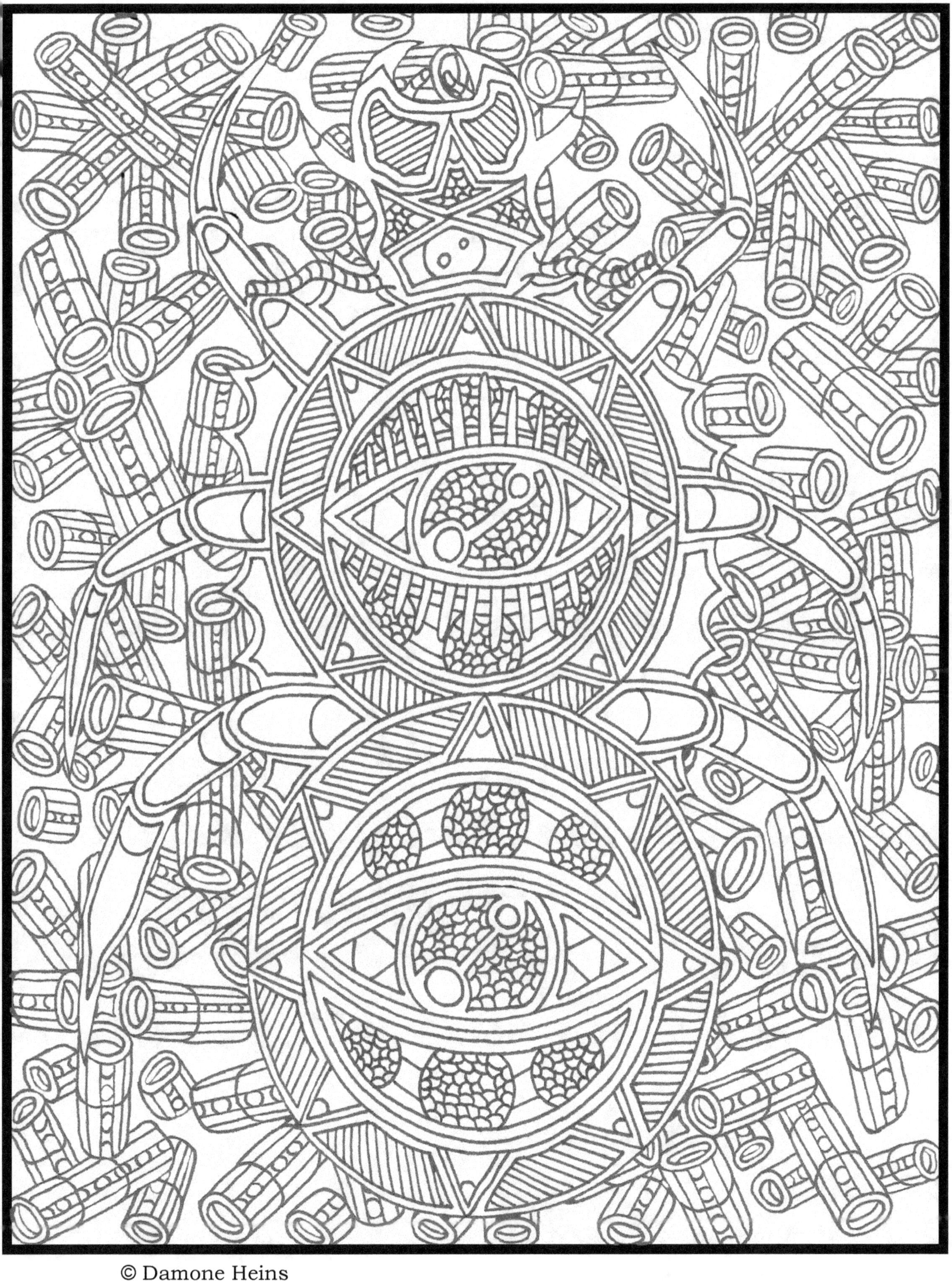

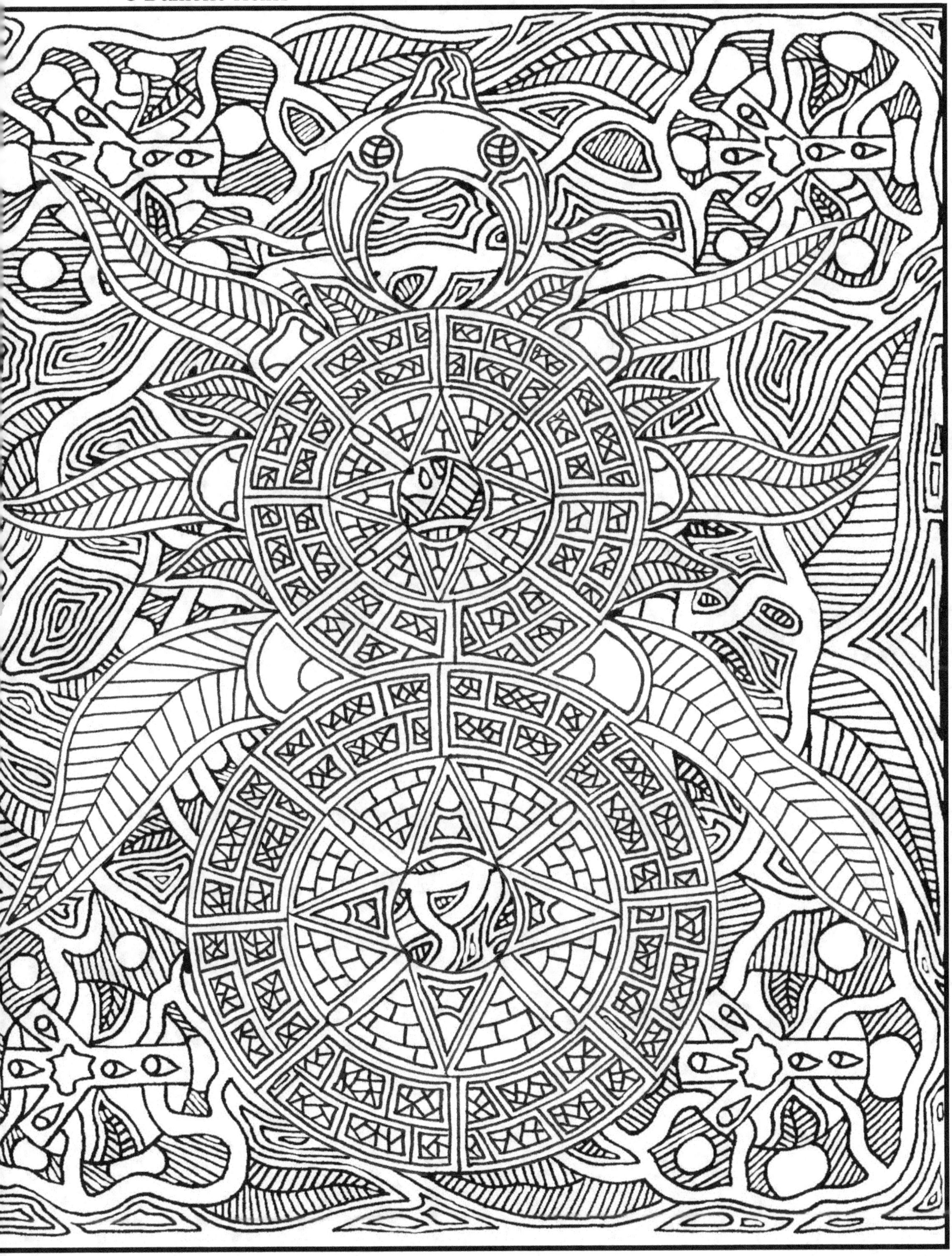

© Damone Heins

© Damone Heins

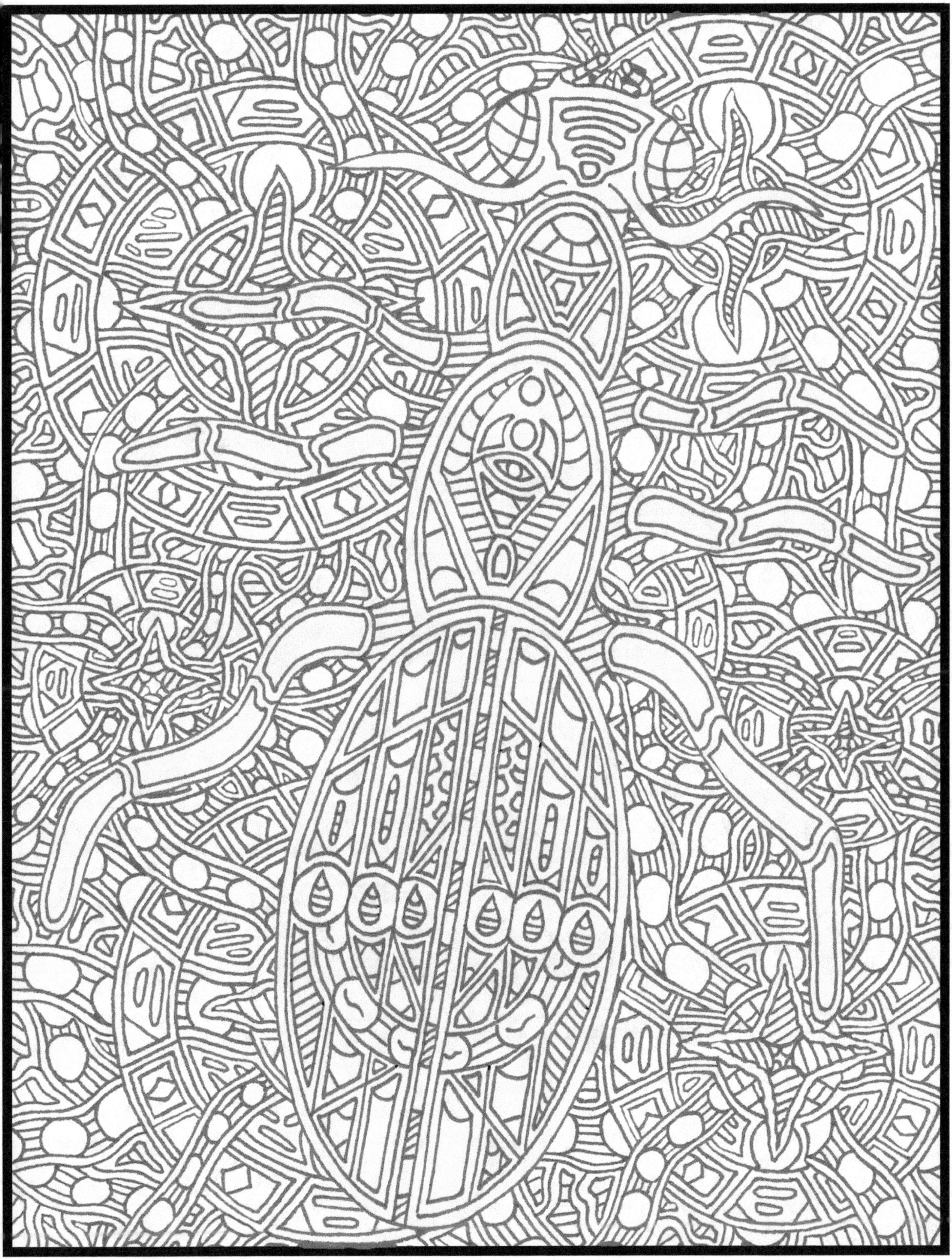

© Damone Heins

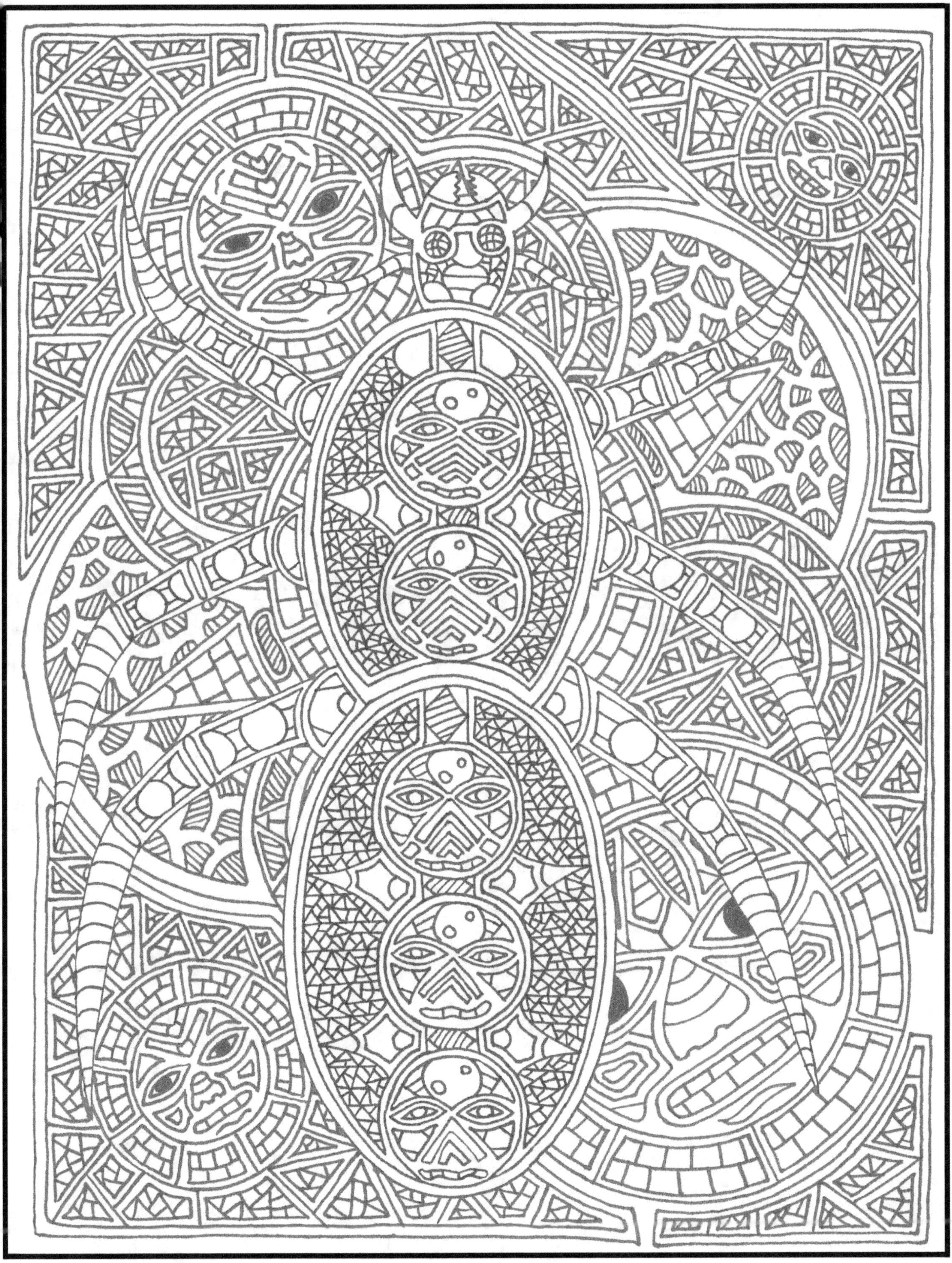

© Damone Heins

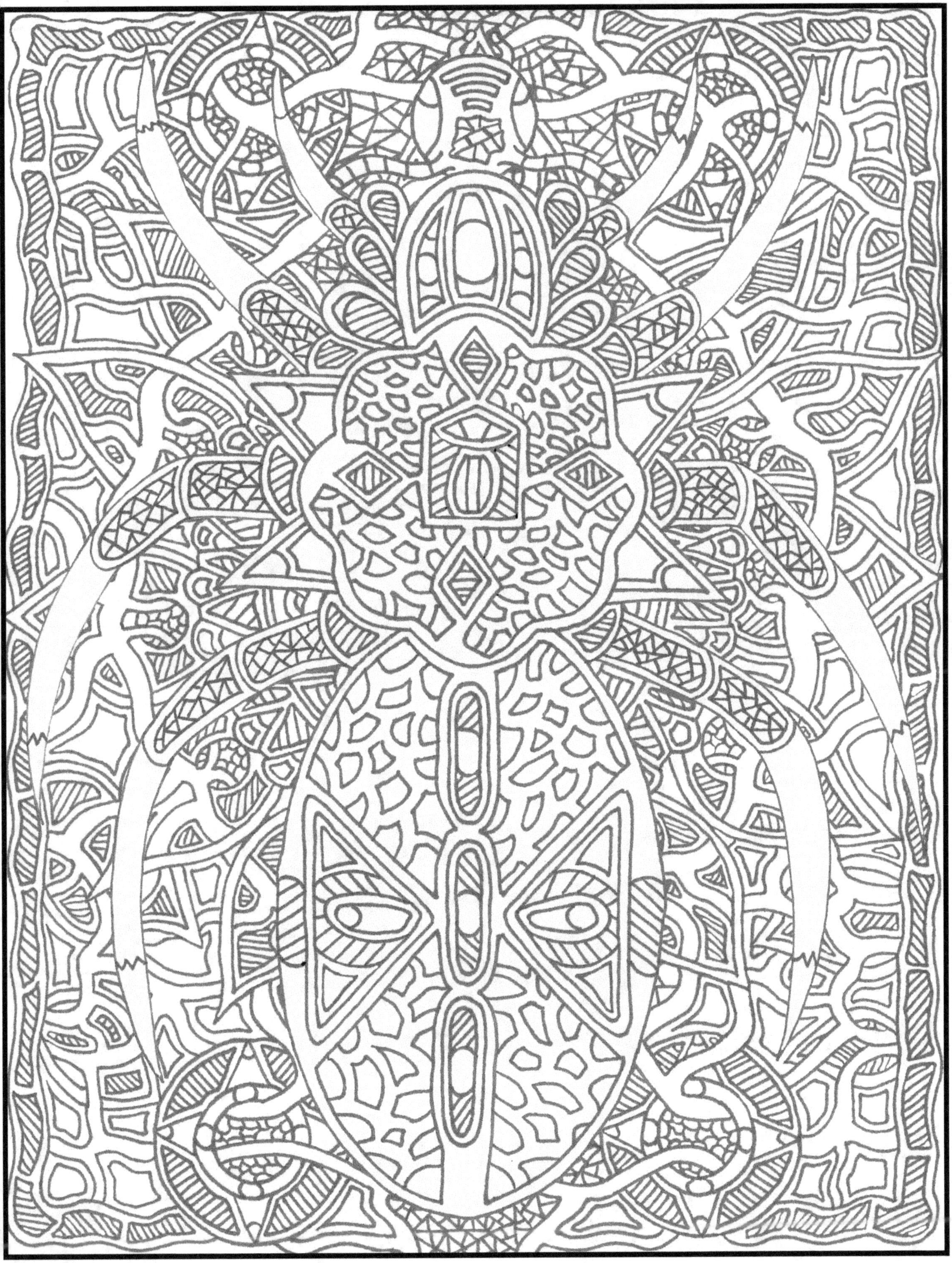

© Damone Heins

© Damone Heins

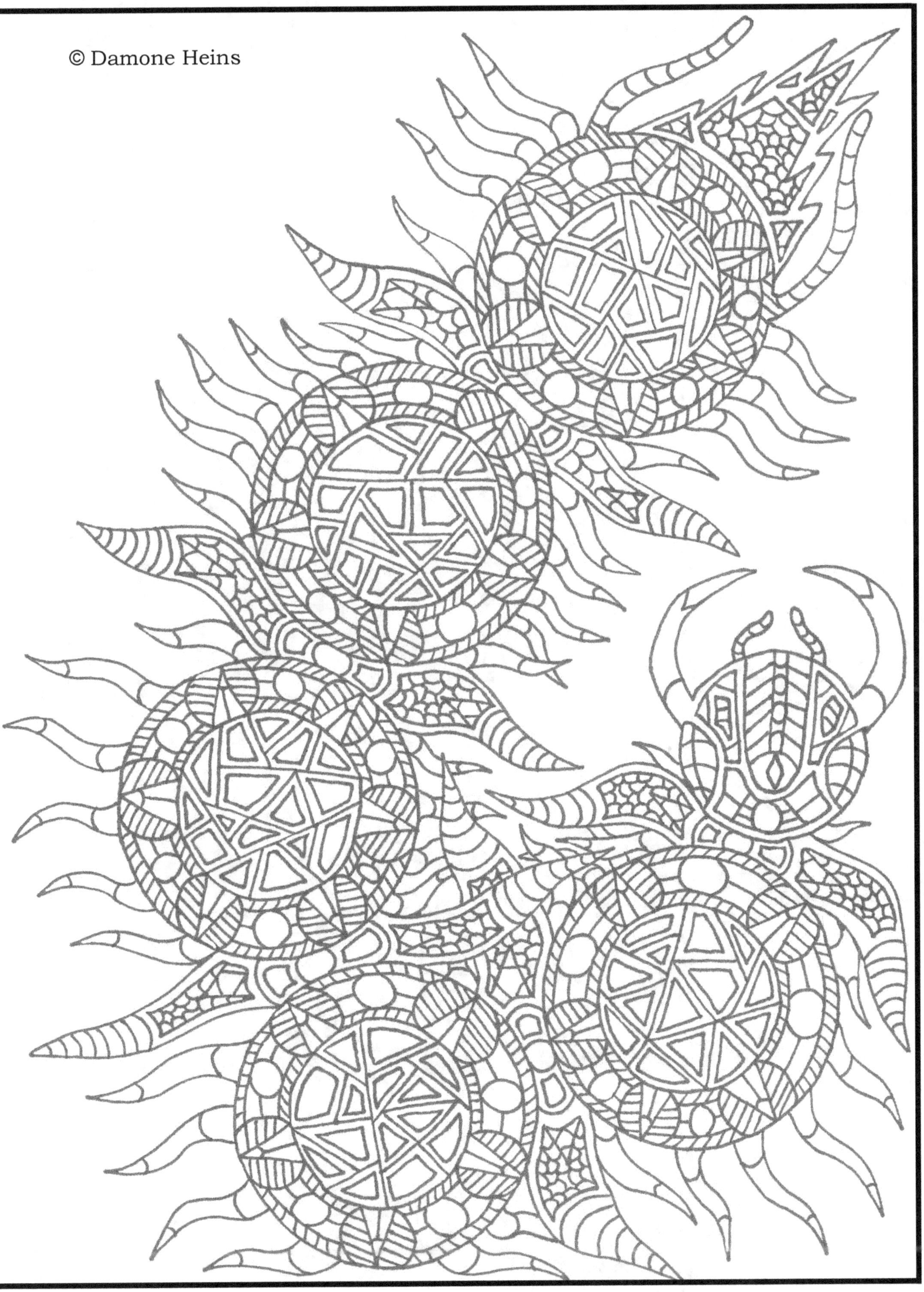

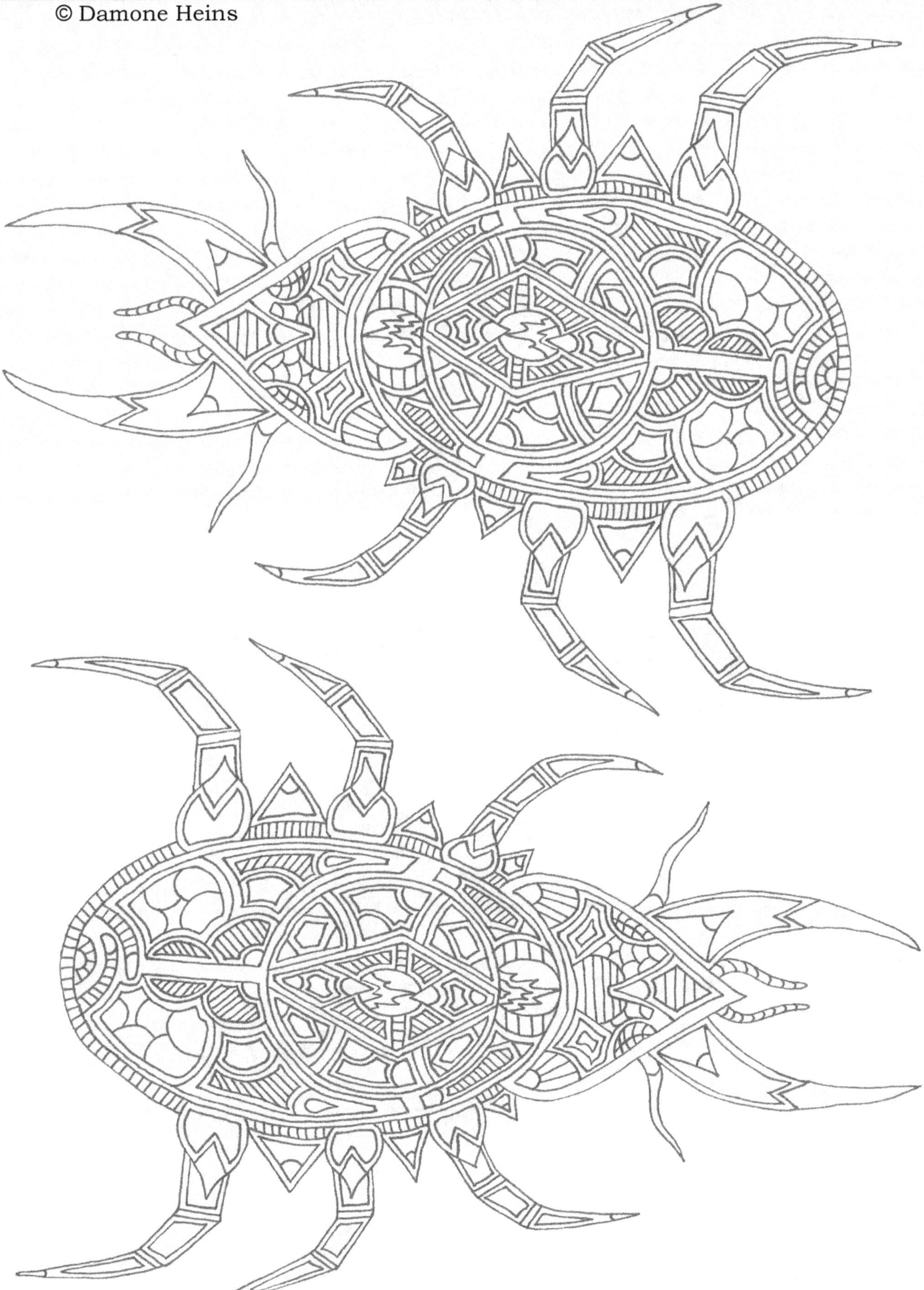

© Damone Heins

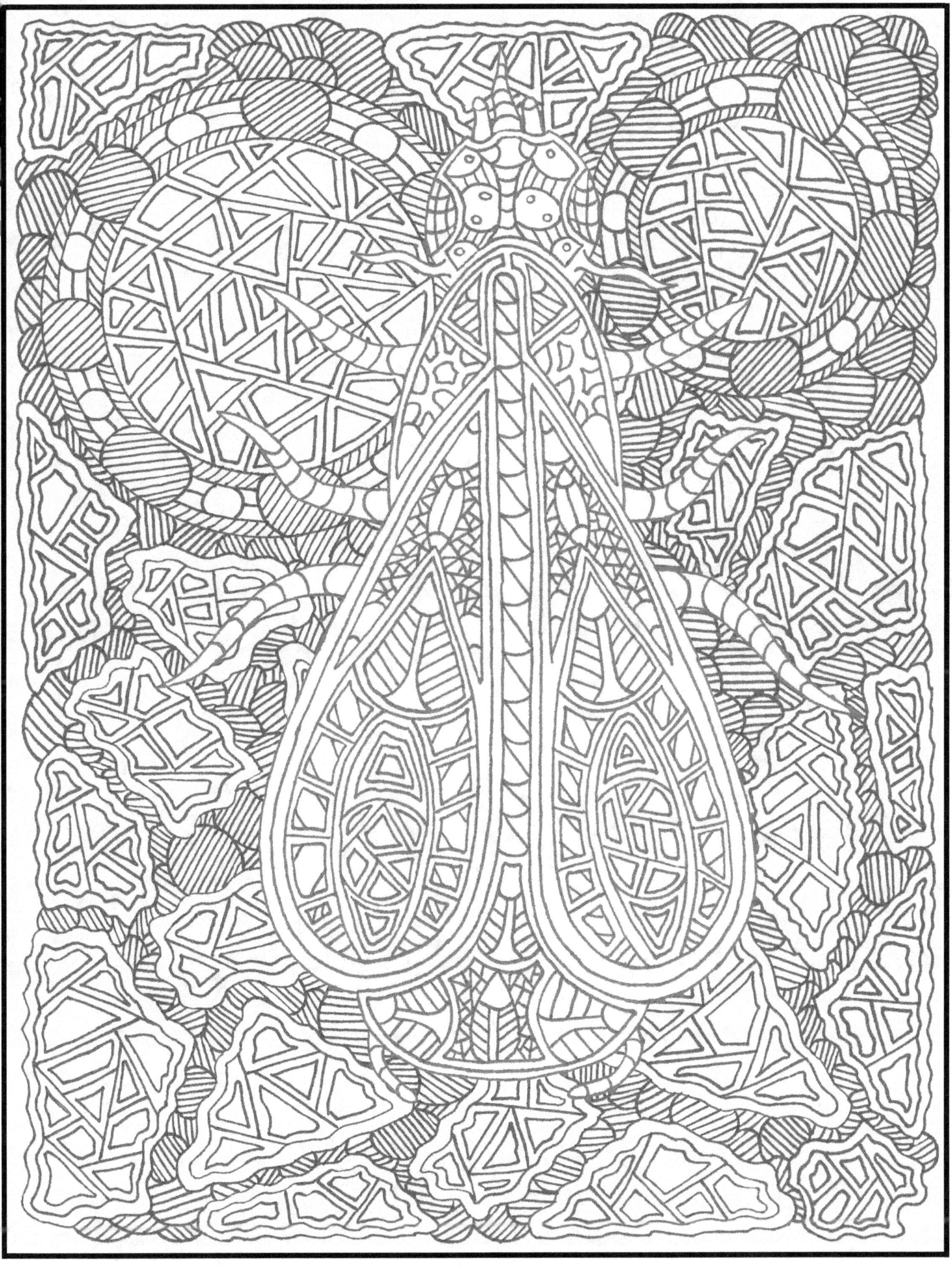

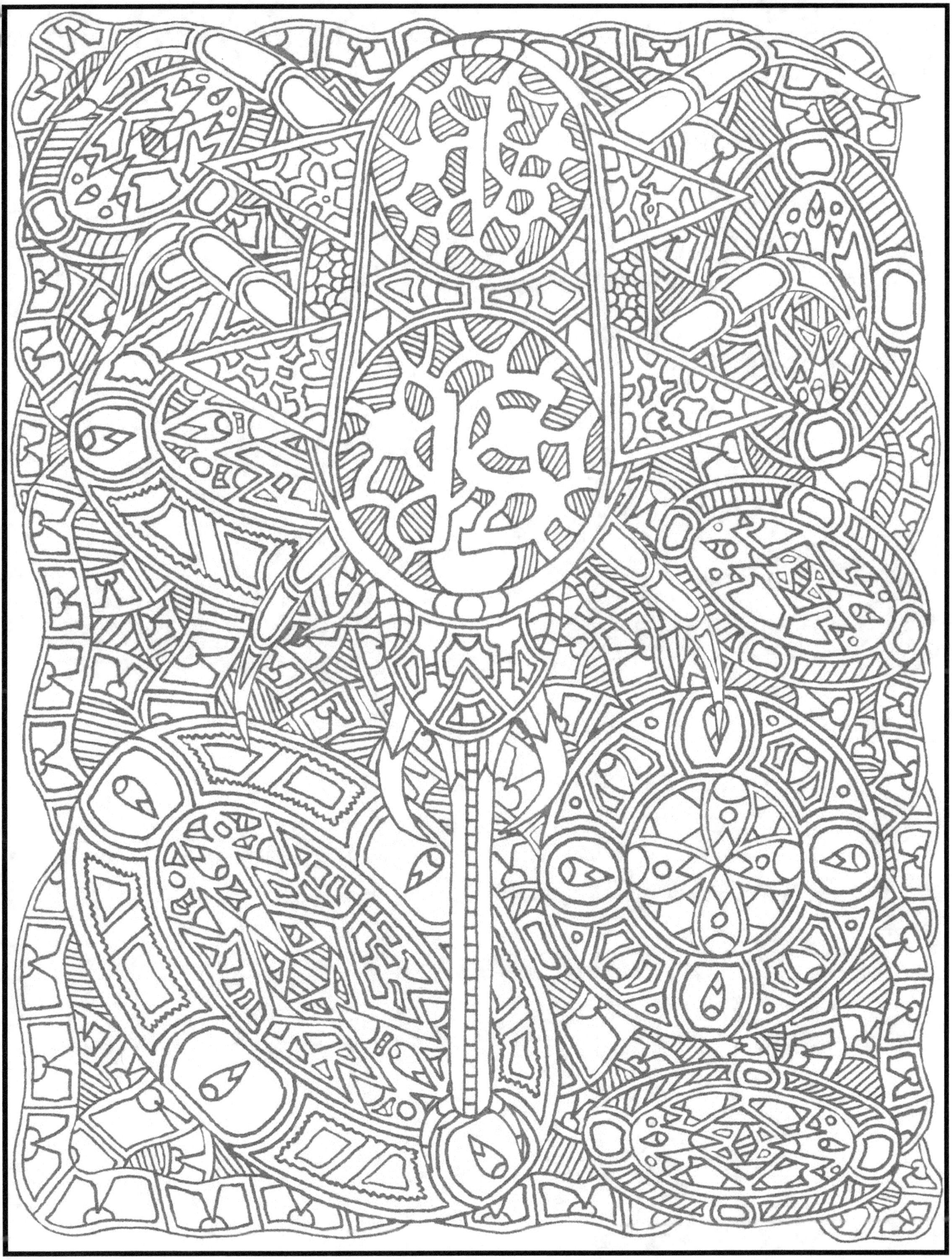

© Damone Heins

© Damone Heins

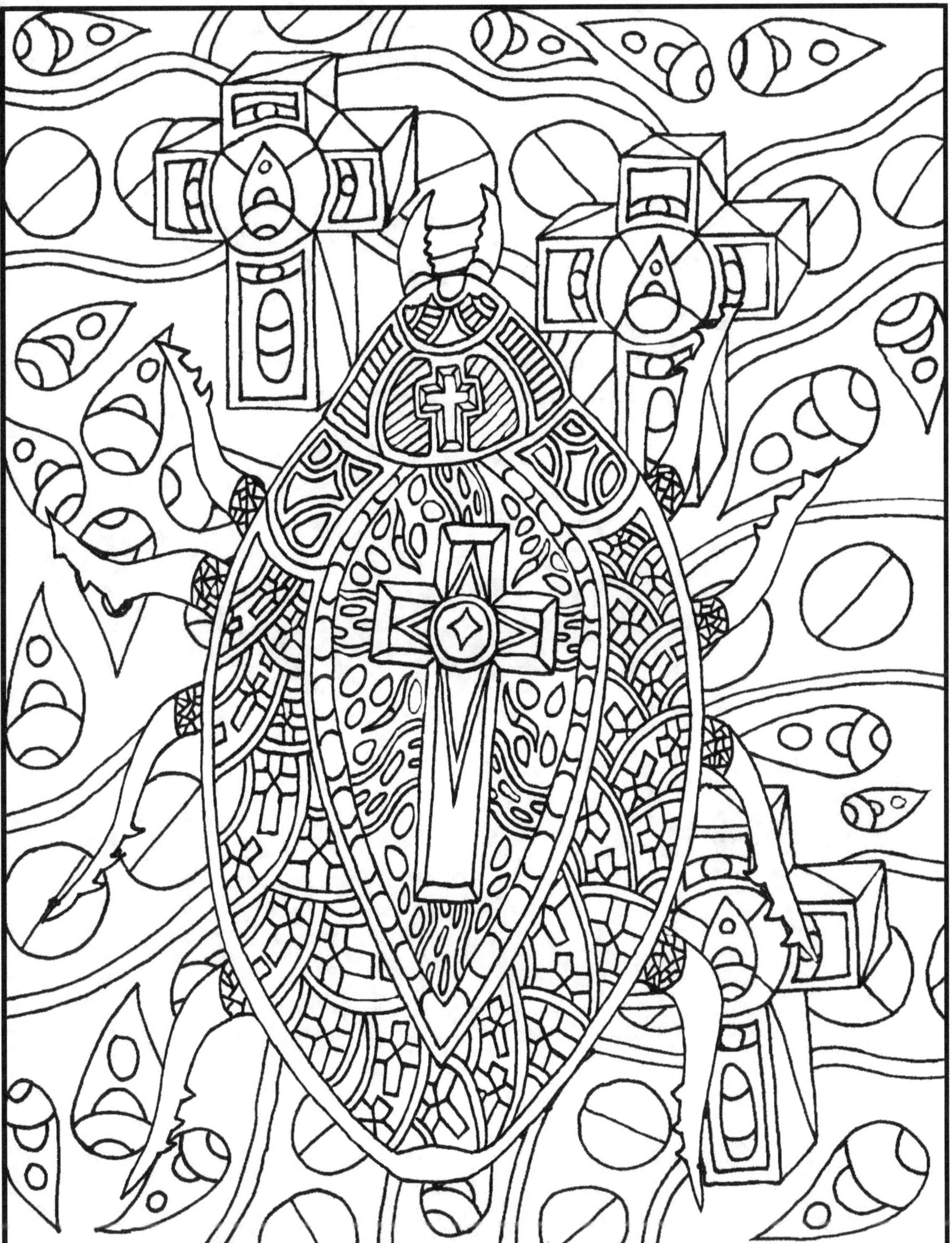

© Damone Heins

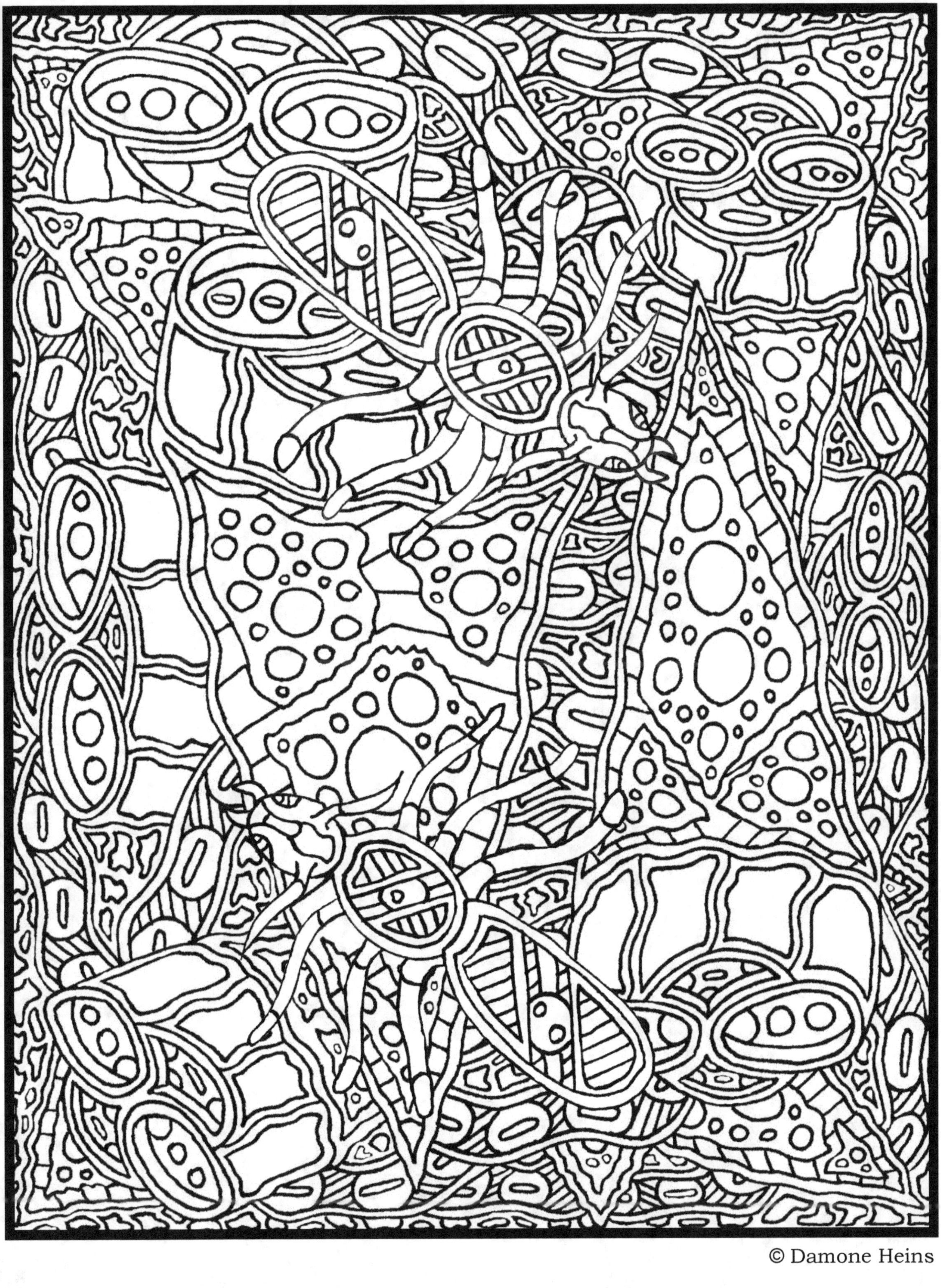

© Damone Heins

© Damone Heins

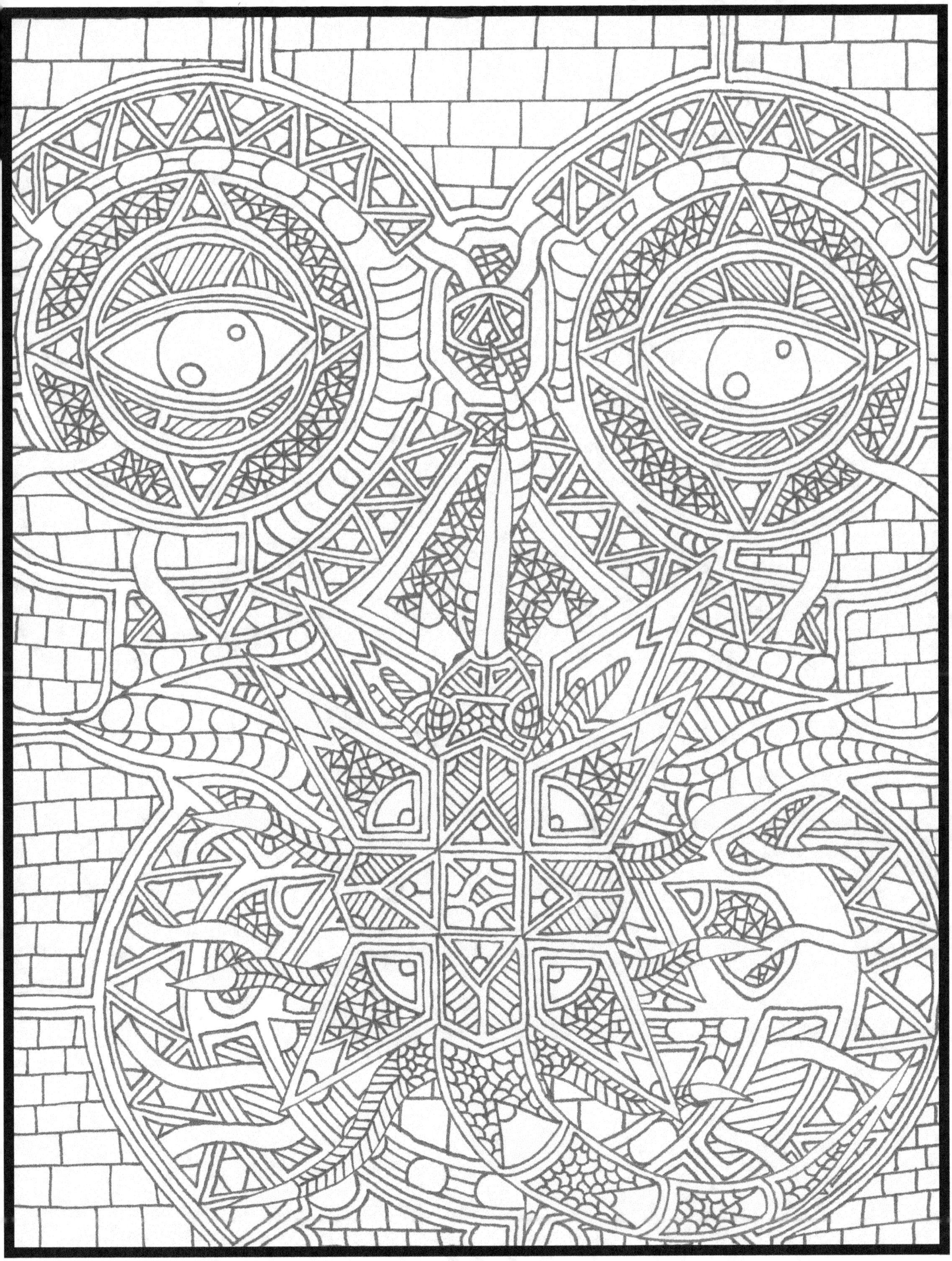

© Damone Heins

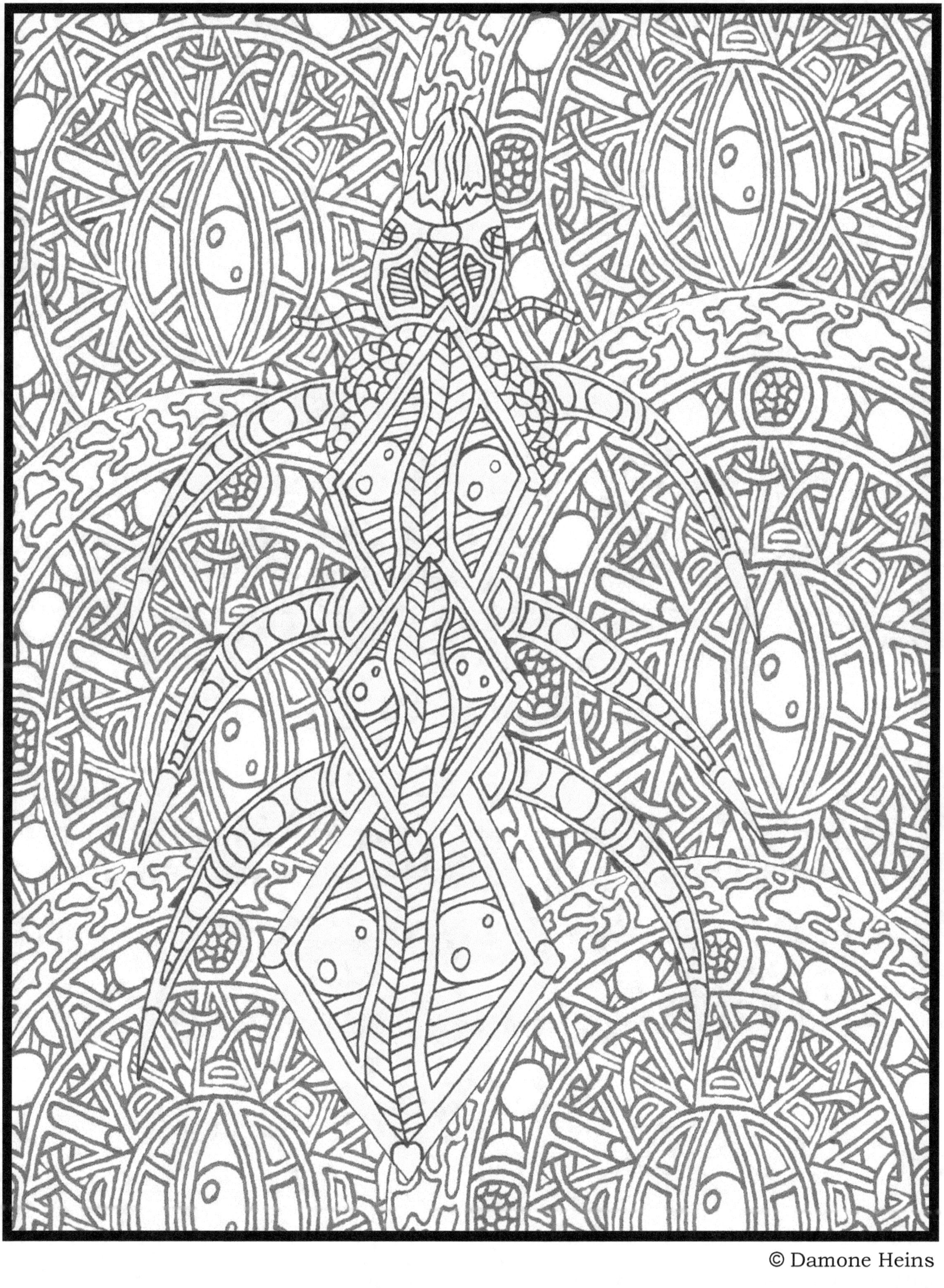

For more books
email me at damonehe@yahoo.com
or mail me at PO. box
2433 Newport Oregon
97365

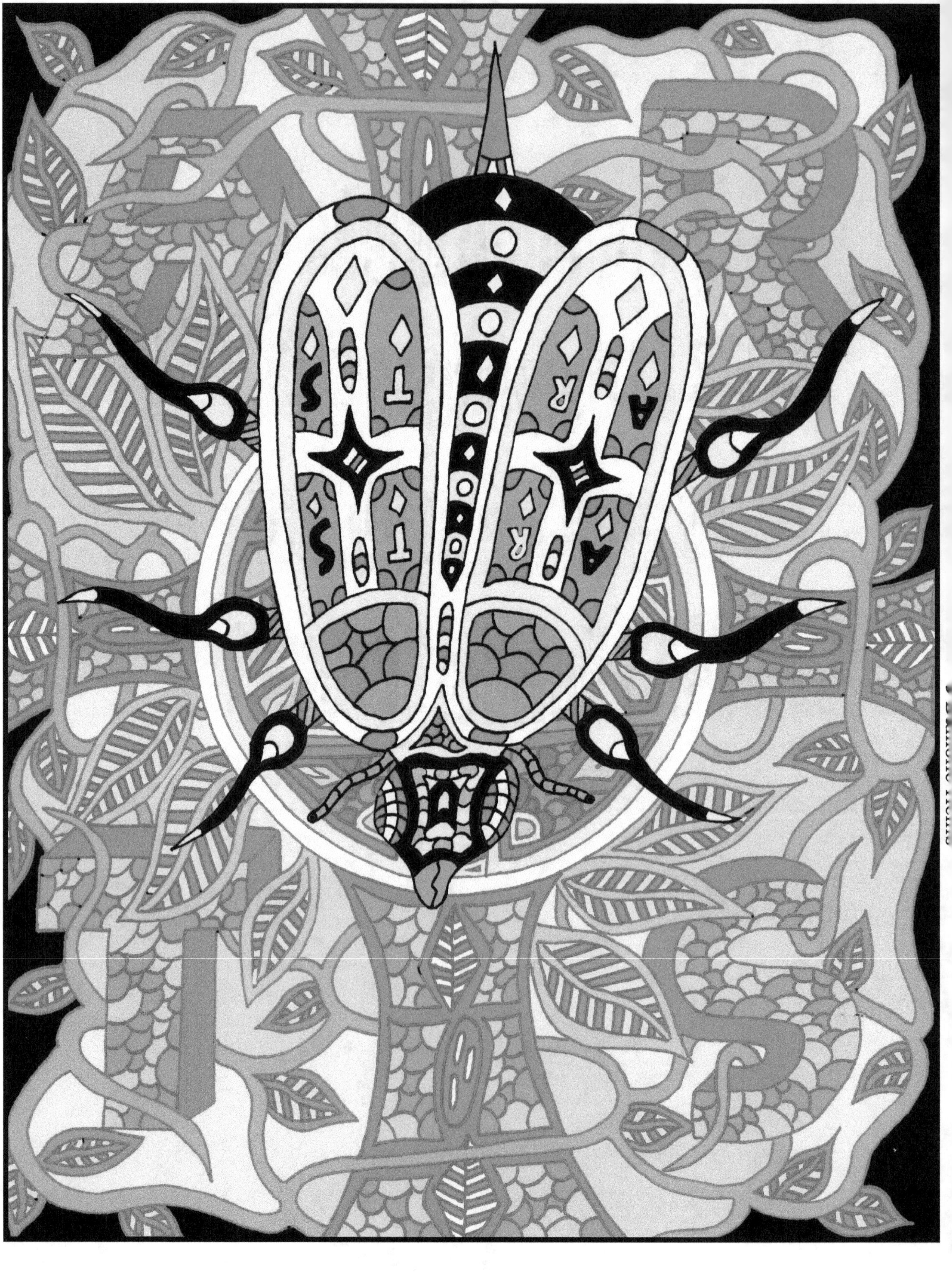

www.ingramcontent.com/pod-product-compliance
Lightning Source LLC
Chambersburg PA
CBHW081855170526
45167CB00007B/3030
* 9 7 8 1 5 4 4 2 3 8 9 0 6 *